Aggregate Supply in the United States: Recent Developments and Implications for the Conduct of Monetary Policy

The collapse of a housing market bubble in the United States and the ensuing financial crisis led to the steepest drop in real GDP and the largest increase in the unemployment rate since the Great Depression. The fallout from these events on credit availability, balance sheets, and confidence continues to weigh on aggregate demand, restraining the pace of recovery in the housing market, firms' willingness to hire and invest, and spending by consumers and state and local governments. In addition, these demand effects have probably diminished the productive capacity of the economy.

In this paper, we examine recent developments in potential output in the United States and discuss the implications for U.S. monetary policy. We begin our analysis by using a standard production-function framework and an unobserved components statistical model to estimate the extent of supply-side damage in recent years, and to identify the components of aggregate supply where the damage has been most acute; this analysis builds on previous work by Fleischman and Roberts (2011) and is similar in spirit to an exercise performed by Kuttner and Posen (2001) to decompose the forces driving Japan's "Lost Decade." Our results suggest that the level of potential GDP was about 6 percent below its pre-crisis trend in 2013:Q1, with a 95 percent confidence interval ranging from 3.8 to 8.1 percent; the model projects the shortfall to widen to 6¾ percent by 2013:Q4. We also show that, in real time, this modeling apparatus would have recognized the decline in potential output relative to its pre-crisis trend only gradually, after some large revisions to the national income and product data had taken place. Although the model has revised down its estimate of potential output since before the crisis, the downside surprise with respect to actual output has been considerably greater; as a result, the model sees actual output as still running significantly below its potential at present.

In terms of the components of aggregate supply, the model estimates the largest losses to be in trend productivity, reflecting both a steep decline in capital accumulation and slower growth in multifactor productivity. However, the natural rate of unemployment also appears to have risen modestly in recently years and the downward trend in labor force participation appears to have steepened, suggesting that the deep recession resulted in some structural damage in the labor market. Motivated by the employment leg of the Federal Reserve's dual mandate, we examine in more detail the evidence pertaining to labor market damage. Our analysis on this point suggests that there has been a modest rise in the natural rate of unemployment and a steepening of the downtrend in labor force participation in recent years, but the evidence is still inconclusive as to how persistent the damage in the labor market will prove to be.

We then examine the implications of these findings for the distinction that is commonly presupposed to exist between "supply" and "demand" aspects of the economy. In many macroeconomic models, aggregate supply shocks are assumed to be exogenous—and specifically as outside the range of influence of monetary policy. However, if some elements of aggregate supply are significantly affected by the condition of aggregate demand, they may also be susceptible to influence from monetary policy. As discussed by Blanchard and Summers (1986), Ball (1999), Kuttner and Posen (2001), and Blanchard (2003) some time ago, and investigated more recently by Stockhammer and Sturn (2012) and Erceg and Levin (2013), demand shocks can have long-lasting effects on unemployment duration and labor force attachment that monetary policy might be able to check. Moreover, monetary policy may be able to influence potential output over the medium term through its effect on new business formation and research and development. Finally, overall aggregate demand clearly influences the supply-side of the economy through business investment and its implications for the pace of capital deepening. In short, through a variety of channels, the distinction between aggregate demand and aggregate supply appears to more blurry than commonly supposed.

In the final section of the paper, we examine the implications of this blurring for the "optimal" conduct of monetary policy. Taken alone, the possibility that potential output will be affected by adverse demand shocks through hysteresis-like effects leads optimal monetary policy to be more activist, in order to mitigate the possible damage to the current and future supply side of the economy. However, other considerations may militate toward restraint in the conduct of monetary policy; these considerations include concerns about the possibility of undermining financial stability or causing inflation expectations to become unmoored. Thus, in an uncertain world, a monetary policymaker's actions will depend not only on the extent to which he or she believes a demand shock is likely to affect potential GDP and employment, but also on his or her view of the risks associated with actively trying to offset these adverse supply-side developments.

I. Recent Supply-Side Developments: Evidence from a State-Space Model

The marked decline in the U.S. unemployment rate from its peak in late 2009 despite only sluggish growth of real GDP, coupled with observations by Cerra and Saxena (2008) and Reinhart and Rogoff (2010) that past financial crises in a variety of countries tended to be followed by persistent shortfalls in real GDP relative to pre-crisis trends, have led many to speculate that the financial crisis and ensuing recession have left a permanent imprint on the productive capacity of the U.S. economy.[2] As a first step in assessing the implications of the

---

[2] See, for example, CBO (2012). Similarly, the European Central Bank (2011) estimates that the financial crisis led to a permanent drop in the level of potential output in the Euro area, but argues that the effects on potential growth going forward are more uncertain. In related work, Martin and Wilson (2013) "find that severe recessions have a sustained and sizable impact on the level of output."

events of recent years for potential output, we examine the behavior of real GDP and unemployment in the context of a simplified version of Okun's Law: $\Delta U = \alpha (\Delta q^* - \Delta q)$, where ΔU is the change in the unemployment rate, Δq and Δq^* are the growth rates of actual and potential GDP, and α is the Okun coefficient, which is currently thought to be about ½ (Ball, Leigh, and Loungani, 2013). With the unemployment rate 2.8 percentage points higher in 2013:Q2 than in 2007:Q4 and real GDP having increased 4.6 percent during that time, this simple rule of thumb suggests that potential output grew about 10 percent over that period, or roughly 1.8 percent per year. This compares with an estimated annual growth rate for potential GDP of 2.7 percent using the same methodology from 2000:Q4 to 2007:Q4.

Of course, this very simple exercise tells us little about the sources of the deceleration in potential GDP over the past five years; nor does it allow for the possibility that the natural rate of unemployment has changed over time; moreover, it assumes that a particularly simple version of Okun's Law holds without error between benchmark dates (for example, 2007:Q4 and 2013:Q2). To allow for a wider array of underlying forces, we employ a richer approach to estimating potential output based on an aggregate production function. This approach allows us to decompose the estimated changes in potential output into changes in potential labor input (including changes in the natural rate of unemployment), capital deepening, and multifactor productivity. To help identify the (unobserved) productive potential of the economy, the model that we use in this estimation exercise incorporates an inflation equation that is similar in spirit to a new-Keynesian Phillips curve, and thus embeds a relationship between economic slack and inflation—concepts that are of central importance to the conduct of monetary policy in the United States.[3]

We use a version of an unobserved components model of the supply-side of the economy developed by Fleischman and Roberts (2011); this model in turn builds on earlier work by Blanchard and Quah (1989), Kuttner (1994), and Basistha and Starz (2008).[4] In particular, we first define (log) output in terms of the components that comprise an aggregate production function:

$$y_t \equiv \Sigma x_{it},$$

where the x_i's include the various determinants of labor input (e.g., population, labor force participation, the employment rate, and the workweek), the factors influencing labor productivity (e.g., capital deepening, labor quality, and multifactor productivity), and a variety of technical factors that account for the different measurement systems used to construct the data series we use in estimation. (In addition, actual output is unobserved in the model but is identified by the comovements of real GDP, real non-farm business output, and real non-farm business income.[5]) We then specify each element of the production function as the sum of a cyclical component, a trend component, and an idiosyncratic residual:

$$x_{it} = \lambda_i(L) \, cyc_t + x_{it}^* + \mu_{it}.$$

Finally, as noted above, we augment the production function equations with a new-Keynesian-style inflation equation. This equation relates current-period inflation to a survey-based measure

---

[3] A production-function approach is also used by the CBO, the IMF, the ECB, and the OECD in developing their estimates of potential output. See also Fernald (2012), Basu and Fernald (2008), Clark (1987), and Gordon (2003).
[4] The state-space model that we use has been embedded in the Federal Reserve's large-scale econometric model of the US economy known as FRB/US. With additional developmental work, partly necessitated by the July 2013 comprehensive revision of the national income and product accounts, the specification of the state-space model within FRB/US has evolved somewhat away from the one we use here.
[5] Nalewaik (2010) shows that elements from the income side of the national income and product accounts have substantial incremental information content relative to elements from the product side.

of long-run inflation expectations, lagged inflation, economic slack (as measured by the same cycle variable that appears in the decomposition of each element of the production function), and changes in the relative prices of energy, food, and imports:

$$\Delta p_t = \omega \Delta p_t^e + (1-\omega)\Delta p_{t-1} + \beta cyc_t + Z_t\Gamma + \varepsilon_t.$$

Our use of a survey-based measure of long-run inflation expectations as an explanatory variable in the equation is motivated by Clark (2011), Del Negro, Giannoni, and Schorfheide (2013), and Ascari and Sbordone (2013), who find that such measures do an excellent job of capturing the low-frequency stochastic trend component of U.S. inflation over the past fifty years.[6]

Following Fleischman and Roberts, we assume that each of the trend variables follows a random walk with drift,

$$x_{it}^* = \alpha_{i,t} + x_{i,t-1}^* + \eta_{it} .$$

For some trend variables (e.g., the natural rate of unemployment) the drift parameter is constrained to equal zero or an estimated constant, but for most trend terms the drift parameter is assumed to follow the AR(1) process $\alpha_{i,t} = .95\,\alpha_{i,t-1} + \varepsilon_{i,t}$. The common cyclical component follows an AR(2) process,

$$cyc_t = \delta_1 cyc_{t-1} + \delta_2 cyc_{t-2} + \xi_t .$$

We use standard maximum likelihood methods for state-space models (specifically, the Kalman filter) to estimate the parameters. (See the appendix for additional details of the model.)

Results from the state-space model based on current-vintage data are shown in Table 1.1 and Figure 1.1. According to the point estimates from the model, as indicated in the top row of the table and the upper-right panel of the figure, potential GDP growth slowed from 2.6 percent

---

[6] From 1990 through the present, Δp_t^e equals the median projection of inflation over the next ten years reported quarterly in the Survey of Professional Forecasters; from 1980 through 1989, it equals the average expected rate of inflation ten years ahead reported in the Hoey survey of financial market participants. Prior to 1980, Δp_t^e is inferred from the low frequency movements in actual inflation.

per year in the 2000-2007 period to 1.3 percent per year on average during the past five years, a somewhat greater stepdown in growth than suggested by the simple Okun's Law calculation above. Moreover, the deceleration in potential GDP is even more pronounced during the past three years, with the average annual change estimated at less than 1 percent. As shown in the upper left panel of Figure 1.1 and the right-most column of Table 1.1, the *level* of potential GDP as of 2013:Q1 is now estimated to be about 6 percent below the trajectory that appeared to be in place based on the average pace of growth estimated over the 2000-2007 period; the model projects the shortfall to widen to 6¾ percent by 2013:Q4.

Although the *level* of potential GDP is now substantially reduced relative to where one would have predicted relative to the pre-crisis trend, its *growth* rate—according to our model—has been less-severely affected, because the model interprets a substantial portion of the hit to potential GDP since 2007 as reflecting one-time adverse shocks to the level of the natural rate, labor force participation, and trend multifactor productivity. (These level shocks are the η_{it} shocks specified above.) Although such level shocks are assumed in the model to have a permanent effect on the level of potential output, they do not affect its expected future growth rate.[7] The importance of this distinction can be seen in line 5 of the table, which reports the estimated growth rate of potential GDP excluding level shocks; this adjusted rate—which represents the model's assessment of the underlying rate of increase in potential GDP once the level shocks have dissipated—is estimated to have slowed somewhat less markedly in recent years. Moreover, a substantial portion of the slowdown in the adjusted growth rate since 2007 reflects an unusually slow pace of capital deepening—a factor whose contribution to growth

---

[7] The $\alpha_{i,t}$ shocks are the primary source of variation in the expected *growth* in potential GDP, with the caveat that persistent movements in the rate of capital deepening can also influence the expected growth rate.

should pick up substantially over time as the recovery in business investment and the broader economy proceeds.

Lines 2 through 4 of the table and the remaining panels of the figure provide some evidence from the model on the sources of the reduction in the potential growth rate of the U.S. economy. The largest contribution to the slowdown in potential output growth is from trend labor productivity (line 3), reflecting both a sharp decline in the contribution to labor productivity from capital deepening (capital services per trend employee hour) and smaller increases in trend multifactor productivity since the financial crisis. The trend growth rate of labor input (line 2) has also slowed in recent years, according to the model, owing to a modest increase in the natural rate of unemployment and a steepening of the trend decline in the labor force participation rate.[8] Even with the estimated slowdown in potential growth, the model's estimate of the cycle (shown in Figure 1.2) is consistent with a sharp drop in resource utilization in 2008 and 2009 and only a gradual and still-incomplete recovery thereafter.

It took some time for these changes to the supply side of the economy to become fully apparent in the data, and consequently many economists did not initially adjust down their estimates of potential output in the United States following the financial crisis despite the international evidence reported by Reinhart and Rogoff (2010) and Cerra and Saxena (2008) for earlier financial crises. To illustrate the discrepancy between the perceived effects of the crisis as they unfolded over time versus how they appear today in hindsight, we estimate the state-space model described above using the data for real activity and inflation that were available in early June of each year between 2007 and 2013, and we use the model to generate estimates of supply-side conditions through the first quarter of the year in question. In addition, for each of

---

[8] Although not explicitly accounted for in the model, some of the steepening in the trend participation rate reflects demographic influences unrelated to the financial crisis or recession. See, for example, Aaronson et al. (2006).

the seven years, we use the estimated model to project the path of potential GDP and the natural rate from the second quarter of the year forward, conditional on the assumption that the contribution of capital deepening to growth would gradually return to its historical average.[9]

The upper two panels of Figure 1.3 present the results of this real-time exercise for the estimated level and rate of change of potential output. Initially, the state-space model did not interpret the available data as suggesting much of a change in the economy's overall productive capacity; in fact, the historical and projected path of potential GDP revised up slightly between the 2008 and 2010 data vintages.[10] However, subsequent data vintages painted a considerably darker picture, and the model's estimates of potential GDP revised down accordingly. Similarly, as illustrated in the lower left panel of Figure 1.3, the model did not initially detect much of an increase in the natural rate of unemployment. Despite all that, and taking into account the vast scale of the recession, the real-time estimates would have proven reasonably accurate in terms of the unemployment gap (lower right panel).[11] Other analysts also marked down their estimates of potential output growth over time, although the timing and the extent of these markdowns varied considerably (see Appendix A.2). [12]

---

[9] Because the state-space model does not forecast capital deepening (in contrast to, say, trend labor force participation), any real-time projection of potential GDP beyond the current quarter requires some assumption for the future path of capital services. Similar considerations apply to population, which in these real-time calculations is assumed to continue rising at the average pace observed over the previous year.

[10] Comparing potential GDP estimates based on the June 2008 and June 2009 vintages of data to those based on subsequent vintages is somewhat difficult because the measures of real output and income used to calculated potential GDP were rebased from 2000 dollars to 2005 dollars beginning in July 2009. In figure 1.3, the 2008 and 2009 real-time estimates of the level of potential GDP are rescaled by a constant multiplicative factor that has the effect of making these vintages' historical estimates of real GDP from the late 1940s through the late 1990s closely match those published at a later date.

[11] The real-time estimates also show a marked revision to the pre-crisis level of the natural rate in 2010. This shift is a result of historical revisions to aggregate output and income released in July 2009, which altered the historical co-movements of these series with the unemployment rate and inflation, thereby resulting in higher estimates of the natural rate beginning back in the late 1990s.

[12] As noted in the appendix, some analysts judgmentally marked down their supply-side estimates in the wake of the financial crisis on the grounds that such events typically result in persistent supply-side damage. Judgmental assessments of this sort raise the question: Should the specification of a "good" state-space model allow for discrete

Of course, considerable uncertainty attends all of these estimates of potential output growth and the natural rate of unemployment. As indicated by the blue shaded region in the upper-right panel of Figure 1.1, the 95 percent confidence band around the state-space model's current estimate of the four-quarter change in potential real GDP is nearly ±1 percentage point, while the comparable confidence band around the estimated natural rate of unemployment (middle-left panel) ranges from about 4½ percent to 7 percent. Moreover, these ranges undoubtedly understate the true uncertainty surrounding our model-based estimates as they do not account for the susceptibility of the data to revision, uncertainty about the specification of the state-space production-function model, or the possibility that other altogether-different frameworks might yield different estimates of supply-side damage. Indeed, one piece of evidence consistent with data-related uncertainty being significant is the fact that in the real-time estimates presented in Figure 1.3, data revisions in 2009 and 2010 accounted for a sizable portion of the downward adjustments to the state-space model's estimates and projections of potential output growth.

II. Evidence from the Labor Market

In this section, we delve more deeply into the possibility of supply-side damage in labor markets, which carry special significance in light of the full-employment leg of the Federal Reserve's dual mandate. Specifically, we provide our take on the evidence regarding three potential sources of labor market damage that have been the focus of much recent commentary: (1) difficulties in reallocating labor across different segments of the economy (industry, occupation, or geographic) associated with the distribution of the demand shock caused by the

---

shifts in parameters and shocks following the onset of a financial crisis? While the answer to this question is almost certainly "yes" in principle, the practical difficulty of doing so is quite high owing to the rarity of such crises domestically and the uncertainties of calibrations based on international experience.

financial crisis and deep recession; (2) a more general deterioration in the efficiency of the matching process between available workers and available jobs; and (3) long-term damage in labor markets (often referred to as hysteresis) associated with the substantial rise in the number of long-term unemployed and a possible reduction in the employability of affected workers.

Reallocation

Given that the financial crisis involved the bursting of a bubble in housing prices and a steep drop in activity that was concentrated in the residential construction sector, it is not surprising that construction employment experienced an outsized decline in late 2007 and 2008 relative to many other industry sectors (Figure 2.1). Similarly, employment in industries tied to housing, including mortgage finance, real estate, and construction-related manufacturing also dropped sharply at the outset of the recession.

It is worth noting, however, that recessions always affect some industries more than others, and in the past these imbalances have typically faded as the overall economy recovered. As shown by the black line in Figure 2.2, the reduction in aggregate activity associated with the financial crisis was initially distributed unevenly and led to a sharp increase in the variance of employment change across broad industry categories in 2008 and 2009.[13] To shed further light on the sources of the rise in dispersion, the blue and green lines in the figure present a decomposition of the variance of the percent changes in employment into two pieces: the part associated with cyclical dynamics (the blue line) and the remainder (the green line).[14] The

---

[13] Specifically, the black line plots the share-weighted variance of the quarterly growth rates of payroll employment across 14 industry categories.

[14] To decompose the variance into its cyclical and noncyclical components, the quarterly percent change in each industry's employment relative to the change in total employment is regressed on a constant term and a measure of the business cycle. Standard variance decomposition methods are then used to decompose the overall variance of industry employment changes into the parts associated with differences in trend growth across sectors, differences in the normal degree of cyclicality across sectors, and differences in the residuals across sectors. The cross-terms that

statistical procedure we use here interprets the overwhelming bulk of the recent spike in total dispersion as cyclical. In contrast, idiosyncratic dispersion increased only moderately during the recession, and by less than it had during several other episodes in the past 50 years. A similar exercise for employment changes across states comes to much the same conclusion (see Valletta and Kuang, 2010).

While Figure 2.2 indicates that the recession did not initially result in an unusual amount of dispersion in employment changes across industries, taking account of the depth of the recession, Figure 2.3 suggests that the industry-specific shocks to labor demand in the recent recession were more persistent than in the past. In particular, this figure plots the variance of the *cumulative* change in industry employment shares for five past recessions from the business cycle peak up to six years after the peak. Consistent with Figure 2.2, the variance of the cumulative changes in employment shares did not look especially unusual during the first few quarters following the most recent cyclical peak; but in subsequent quarters, the cumulative variance rises sharply, and by two years out is well above that following any of the earlier business cycle peaks. Thus, the most recent recession may have generated a need for a more significant amount of labor reallocation than did earlier recessions.[15]

These measures of sectoral imbalances rely on fairly aggregate industry or geographic definitions and thus may be too crude to capture the full extent of the reallocation across more-narrowly-defined industries, occupations, or geographic areas that was engendered by the financial crisis. An alternative way to assess sectoral reallocation is to focus on permanent job

---

include the cyclical term are allocated to the variance associated with the business cycle. Other cross-terms are allocated to the idiosyncratic variance.

[15] In computing the variance of the cumulative changes in industry employment shares, we first removed the long-run trends in the shares using a Hodrick-Prescott filter with λ set equal to 1,024,000 (so that we only removed the very long-run trends). Without detrending, the variances from the 2007 peak are still generally above those in the earlier periods two to three years out, but fall below the dispersion in employment shares following the 1981 peak after about four years.

loss more generally, on the grounds that permanent separations of any type are potentially associated with substantial costs in terms of relocation and lost human capital that could slow the pace at which workers find new jobs.[16] Figure 2.4 shows that the rate of permanent job loss— the red line—rose sharply during the recession, briefly reaching a level about half again as high as it had reached in the aftermath of the relatively mild recession during the early 2000s and a little higher than it had reached during the 1982 recession. Although the rate of permanent job loss has trended downward during the past four years and is currently close to its pre-recession level, the *stock* of persons still unemployed following a permanent job loss (the black line) remains noticeably higher than prior to the recession. This suggests that many permanent job losers continue to experience difficulties in finding a new job, consistent with the hypothesis that structural unemployment may still be elevated.[17] That said, the stock of permanent job losers has now moved down about half way to its precession level—roughly proportionate to the improvement in overall unemployment since its peak—and it seems likely that further improvements in economic activity and job opportunities will lead to further reductions.

Matching efficiency and the Beveridge Curve

Proponents of the view that the rate of structural unemployment has risen also point to the Beveridge curve—the relationship between the unemployment rate and job vacancies—as

---

[16] See, for example, Loungani and Rogerson (1989) and Figura and Wascher (2010). In addition, the need to reallocate physical or organizational capital can lead to reductions in productivity and higher unemployment, especially if the displaced capital is highly specific to the affected industry or firm (Ramey and Shapiro, 2001).
[17] Two potential sources of a continued elevated stock of permanent job losers are a reduction in labor mobility as a result the sharp drop in house prices and associated increase in homeowners who are "underwater" and the possibility that displaced workers would resist lower wage offers (wage rigidity). Researchers who have studied housing markets and migration have thus far found little empirical support for an effect of house lock on labor mobility (see, for example, Molloy, Smith, and Wozniak, 2013; and Valletta, 2013). There is less evidence on the effect of wage rigidity on the speed of labor reallocation in recent years, although Daly et al. (2013) find that downward nominal wage rigidity increased during the recession.

evidence for this view.[18] Through long stretches of time, the vacancy rate and the

unemployment rate have traced out a seemingly stable schedule that is often interpreted as

reflecting changes in aggregate demand playing out in the context of a labor market exhibiting

roughly constant structural unemployment. As shown in Figure 2.5, which measures job

vacancies using data from the "Job Openings and Labor Turnover Survey" or JOLTS, the data

points from late 2000 through 2008 represented one such period in which the Beveridge curve

appeared to be stable. Beginning in mid-2009, however, it became apparent that the Beveridge

curve had shifted to the right. During the past four years, the vacancy rate has been rising and

the unemployment rate has been falling, consistent with the usual negative relationship between

these two series, but the locus of points traced out has been distinctly to the right of the one that

prevailed during the 2000s.

It would be tempting to conclude from the rightward shift in the Beveridge curve that

structural unemployment increased in the aftermath of the financial crisis and the onset of the

ensuing recession—and that may ultimately prove to be the right conclusion. But before

drawing that conclusion, it is important to note that the Beveridge curve can shift for a variety of

reasons, some of which are cyclical rather than structural in nature.[19] Indeed, as the labor market

has improved following past recessions, the vacancy-unemployment locus has typically

exhibited a counter-clockwise loop (that is, unemployment has eventually declined more than

would be apparently consistent with the normal stable downward-sloping schedule). One factor

that could generate such looping behavior is extended unemployment insurance benefits. All

---

[18] See, for example, Hassett (2013). The use of the Beveridge Curve to help distinguish between structural and cyclical increases in unemployment was also prominent in the debate between Lilien (1982) and Abraham and Katz (1986).
[19] See Diamond (2013) for an extensive treatment of the Beveridge Curve and a discussion of the relevance of the recent evidence for assessing the extent to which the currently high level of unemployment is structural or cyclical in nature.

else equal, when extended UI benefits become available, some unemployed individuals may experience a reduction in the incentive to maintain their intensity of job search, and others who would otherwise have dropped out of the labor force may be induced to report themselves as unemployed (and undertake sufficient search to qualify as such) in order to receive benefits. For both reasons, the measured unemployment rate associated with any given job vacancy rate may increase.[20] During the recovery phase, as the availability of extended UI benefits is curtailed and eventually eliminated, the process unwinds, and the unemployment rate comes down by more than one would predict based only on the job vacancy rate. In the most recent episode, extended UI benefits began becoming broadly available in late 2008. During the past two years, however, availability of extended UI benefits has been greatly curtailed, with the number of recipients now down to about one quarter of its peak. Despite that fact, as can be seen in the figure, there is still only the faintest suggestion in the most recent few datapoints that the Beveridge curve may have begun to shift back to the left.[21,22]

Of course, there may also be movements in the Beveridge curve that represent changes in the efficiency of the job matching process more broadly (that is, not specifically associated with

---

[20] Some recent evidence on this point is provided by Farber and Valletta (2013), who find that extended UI benefits reduced the exit rate from unemployment and increased the duration of unemployment spells. They also find that the effect on unemployment exit and duration stemmed primarily from a reduction in exits from the labor force rather than from a decrease in the job finding rate.

[21] In addition, Davis, Faberman, and Haltiwanger (2012) argue that persistently weak demand has caused employers to be more selective in choosing whom to hire, resulting in a decrease in the ratio of hires to vacancies and thus an outward shift in the Beveridge Curve without an increase in structural unemployment (assuming that the effect fades as real activity recovers).

[22] Other analysts (for example, Lazear and Spletzer (2012); Sahin et al., (2012)) have constructed measures of mismatch from disaggregated unemployment and vacancy data. The Lazear-Spletzer and Sahin et al. measures of industrial mismatch rose sharply during the recession but began to fall back in 2010 and by early this year were at or close to their levels prior to the recession—a development that Lazear and Spletzer interpreted as suggesting "that changes in industrial mismatch are cyclical, rather than structural." Their occupational mismatch indexes show a similar pattern, although the Sahin et al. measure is still a little on the high side. In contrast, Sahin et al. find essentially no evidence that geographic mismatch (not shown in the figure) increased during the recession or that it is currently above normal levels. We thank Aysegul Sahin for providing updated estimates of the mismatch indices presented in Sahin et al.

occupational, industry, or geographic mismatch), and which could be viewed as stemming from a change in structural unemployment. In this regard, Barnichon and Figura (2013) propose a model that attempts to decompose movements in the Beveridge curve into various components and, in particular, to isolate the part of the outward shift that is associated with a decline in matching efficiency.[23] As indicated in Figure 2.6, the estimates from this model suggest that structural unemployment increased by nearly 1½ percentage points between the onset of the recession and the end of 2011. However, the model also suggests that matching efficiency may have begun to improve more recently, although it remains well below where it was prior to the recession. Using a somewhat different framework, Daly et al. (2012) combine the Beveridge curve with a job creation curve and estimate that the natural rate of unemployment was about 6 percent at the end of 2011, about 1 percentage point above its level prior to the recent recession.

Hysteresis

An important and unusual aspect of the recent recession and the subsequent slow recovery—and one that heightens the risk that structural labor market damage may have been sustained already or may yet emerge—is the sharp increase in long-term unemployment since the onset of the financial crisis. As shown in Figure 2.7, the number of individuals unemployed for more than 26 weeks as a share of the labor force rose to 4.3 percent in April 2010 and has since fallen only to 2.7 percent, as compared with ¾ percent in 2007; likewise the share of the unemployed who have been out of work more than 26 weeks (not shown in the figure) peaked at about 45 percent in early 2011 and remains above one-third today, well above the levels experienced during any previous post-World War II recession. Long-term unemployment is of

---

[23] To calculate their measure of matching efficiency, Barnichon and Figura regress the job-finding rate of the unemployed on the ratio of vacancies to unemployment. The residuals from the regression represent shifts in the Beveridge curve associated with changes in the efficiency of job matching.

particular concern because individuals out of work for extended periods of time may find that their skills, reputations, and networks deteriorate, resulting in a persistently higher level of structural unemployment or a steeper downtrend in the labor force participation rate. Although such effects do not appear to have been important in the United States in the past, they have been evident in other advanced economies, and the unprecedented durations of unemployment during the present episode in the United States may reduce the relevance of historical experience in this country.

It is well known that individuals with longer spells of unemployment find it more difficult to become reemployed. For example, as indicated in Figure 2.9, job finding rates for the long-term unemployed are nearly always well below those for individuals with shorter unemployment spells. In the past, however, researchers have found it difficult to separate the effects of unobserved heterogeneity in the individuals experiencing long spells of unemployment from duration dependence. To address this issue, Kroft, Lange, and Notowidigdo (2013) recently conducted an experiment and found that, all else equal, potential employers were much less likely to call back job applicants with longer spells of unemployment than otherwise identical applicants with shorter spells, evidence that is consistent with duration dependence in unemployment. Although the aggregate implications of this finding are unclear, under some interpretations employers' aversion to long unemployment spells could result in hysteresis.

If hysteresis-type effects were taking hold, one might expect to see an improvement in the job-finding rates for the unemployed with shorter durations but not for those with longer spells of unemployment. Thus far, the evidence on this point seems mixed. As shown in Figure 2.8, job-finding rates have edged up, on balance, in recent years for those unemployed less than 27 weeks and by more than the job finding rates for the longer-term unemployed.

However, the differences are not large and the data on these flows are fairly noisy. At the same time, as indicated in Figure 2.9, the rate of exit from the labor force among the long-term unemployed has risen since late 2009, but broadly speaking, no more than has the rate for those with shorter unemployment spells; moreover, this upward drift reverses an earlier move in the other direction--a pattern that seems consistent with the variation during this time in the availability of extended unemployment insurance benefits.

There have also been some concerns that the availability of disability insurance (DI) would induce a larger number of those with poor job prospects to permanently leave the labor force—concerns that were based in part on evidence that those receiving disability payments tend to remain out of the labor force until retirement (Autor and Duggan, 2006). However, as indicated in Figure 2.10, the proportion of DI recipients has deviated only slightly in recent years from its longer-term upward trend. In addition, Mueller, Rothstein, and von Wachter (2013) find little evidence that the expiration of UI benefits causes individuals to move onto DI rolls. That said, applications for disability insurance have risen noticeably in recent years and, if approved, this bulge in applications could cause cyclically-induced exits from the labor force to become permanent.

Inflation

Finally, some observers point to the absence of an ongoing steep deceleration in wage and price inflation as evidence that there must have been a noticeable increase in structural unemployment.[24] However, the results from the state-space model provide another interpretation, namely that changes in inflation are less informative about labor market slack (and

---

[24] See, for example, Gordon (2013), who argues that the relationship between short-run unemployment and inflation has been stable in recent years, and thus that the sharp rise in long-term unemployment represents an increase in structural unemployment.

resource utilization more generally) than in the 1970s and 1980s because of the substantial

flattening of the Phillips curve over the past two decades. Moreover, other factors, such as

downward nominal wage rigidity and well-anchored inflation expectations, appear to be more

likely explanations for the recent behavior of wages and prices. For example, Daly et al. (2013)

present a model in which downward nominal wage rigidity reduces the responsiveness of wage

inflation to the unemployment gap (thus flattening the Phillips curve).[25] They then show that the

behavior of wages since 2007 is well explained by the model given the sizable degree of

downward nominal wage rigidity observed during this period. Similarly, Del Negro, Giannoni,

and Schorfheide (2013) show that in a standard DSGE model with a significant degree of price

rigidity, inflation expectations remain fairly stable, causing inflation to depend more on expected

future marginal costs than on economic slack. Of course, the stability of long-run inflation

expectations is not a fundamental property of the economy that monetary authorities can exploit

forever, but rather something that can be taken advantage of only cautiously and only for a time

(although that time could be quite long).

Summing up

We see the evidence of recent years as suggesting that the natural rate of unemployment

may have moved up between ½ and 1½ percentage points since the onset of the recent recession,

roughly in line with the estimates from the state-space model. In addition, while the labor force

participation is clearly on a longer-run downtrend caused by the aging of the U.S. population, it

seems likely that at least some of the currently low level of the participation rate is associated

---

[25] As these authors note, this research builds on previous work by Tobin (1972) and Akerlof, Dickens, and Perry (1996).

with weak aggregate demand.[26] However, the evidence also suggests that the factors leading to these forms of deterioration in the labor market have begun to reverse and that further increases in aggregate demand will likely bring about further healing in the labor market. But at the same time, we cannot rule out a darker possibility, namely that hysteresis effects associated with the continued high level of long-term unemployment could lead to permanent damage in the productivity or employability of those who remain willing to work, and could lead others to throw in the towel and permanently exit the labor force.

III. The Potential Endogeneity of Recent Supply-Side Developments

Although considerable uncertainty attends any estimate of potential output and employment, the preceding analysis strongly suggests that the U.S. economy has experienced significant supply-side damage since 2007; broadly speaking, these results are consistent with the now-conventional claim that major financial crises tend to reduce a nation's productive potential. However, we argue in this section that the implications for monetary policy may differ sharply from what is commonly presumed because much of the supply-side damage could be an endogenous response to weak aggregate demand. If so, then an activist monetary policy may be able to limit the amount of supply-side damage that occurs initially, and potentially may also help to reverse at a later stage a portion of such damage as does occur. By themselves, such considerations militate toward a more aggressive stance of policy and help to buttress the case for a highly aggressive policy response to a financial crisis and associated recession. In section 4, we discuss other considerations that may incline policymakers toward a less aggressive policy response.

---

[26] There is a wide range of views as to how much of the decline in participation in recent years reflects cyclical influences. In particular, Erceg and Levin (2013) estimate that cyclical factors account for about 2 percentage points of the decline in labor force participation since 2007, while Aaronson, Davis, and Hu (2012) put the cyclical decline at roughly 1 percentage point, and Hornstein (2013) finds only a small participation rate gap at present.

Contrasting views

In setting monetary policy, central banks have traditionally tried to distinguish between trend and cyclical movements by disentangling the effects of exogenous "supply" shocks (which are assumed to influence the economy's long-run equilibrium) from the effects of "demand" shocks (which are assumed to drive the economy away from its steady state). The rationale for this distinction is presumably rooted at least partly in the assumed long-run neutrality of monetary policy: However important it may be in influencing the paths of real variables in the short run, monetary policy cannot affect output, employment, or unemployment once prices have fully adjusted and the effects of other nominal rigidities have faded away. For this reason, monetary policymakers have to accept the real long-run equilibrium of the economy as something that is determined outside the sphere of monetary influence, and they need to recognize that it would be fruitless or even outright damaging to seek a different set of real outcomes. (See Barro and Gordon, 1983.)

The standard textbook presentation of a vertical Phillips Curve has this flavor: In the long run, output must return to a level that is determined by the location of the vertical aggregate supply curve, and is invariant with respect to the conduct of monetary policy. The aggregate demand curve may be buffeted by factors over time, including the stance of monetary policy, but in the long run, the location of the aggregate demand curve matters only for the value of the equilibrium real interest rate consistent with stable inflation.[27]

---

[27] Dornbusch and Fischer (1978), the first edition of their macro text, describes the expectations-augmented Phillips curve in this manner (pp. 404-405) and specifically references a long-run vertical Phillips curve (page 410). For the first known presentation of the standard textbook vertical supply curve to the Federal Open Market Committee, see page 25 of the document provided at:
http://www.federalreserve.gov/monetarypolicy/files/FOMC19831115material.pdf. To be sure, ideas along these lines had been presented and discussed among Federal Reserve staff for more than a decade, as illustrated by an "accelerationist" version of the Board's MPS model developed by William Poole (1971) and a paper that Robert Lucas gave at a 1971 conference hosted at the Board (Lucas, 1972).

While the sharp separation between supply shocks and demand shocks—and the identification of the first with circumstances that monetary policymakers must accept as given and the second as factors that they may be able to usefully counteract—is characteristic of particularly simple models, it greatly oversimplifies the real world. As Blanchard and Summers (1986) noted many years ago in the European context, weak real activity may give rise to long-lived hysteresis effects in labor markets, thereby providing a strong motivation for governments to implement policies (fiscal or otherwise) to both check the magnitude of economic downturns and so limit the supply-side damage that occurs, and to later boost the pace of activity as the economy recovers to repair whatever damage has occurred. Ball (1999) subsequently expanded on this idea by examining cross-country evidence on the role of monetary policy in influencing the magnitude of unemployment hysteresis effects, and concluded that policy-related supply-side effects were substantial for many European economies—a conclusion that has been reaffirmed in empirical work by Stockhammer and Sturn (2012).

We would go beyond this literature, however, and argue that the potential endogeneity of supply-side developments extends well beyond the labor market, and includes such factors as multifactor productivity and capital deepening. To this end we review below several mechanisms that all have the characteristic of blurring the distinction between supply and demand, and therefore prompt a careful consideration of the factors that monetary policy must accommodate versus those it can counteract.

Before describing these mechanisms, we should note that the statistical methods commonly used to distinguish "cycle" from "trend" may exacerbate the blurring problem in severe recessions and slow recoveries. Most if not all of these statistical methods identify the "trend" with low-frequency movements in the variables of interest; the remaining movements are assumed to be cycle or noise. In a typical model of this type, the dividing line between "cyclical" frequencies and "trend" frequencies is generally something like five or six years. That distinction may be appropriate for the dynamics of most recessions, but the adjustment of labor force participation, the unemployment rate, and productivity to the events of the last few years arguably will play out over an even longer span of time. For example, the recession and slow recovery may impair job matching and other aspects of labor market functioning for quite a few years. Moreover, these same conditions may lead a significant number of older workers to drop out of the labor force permanently at an earlier age than otherwise would have occurred, thereby depressing the participation rate for possibly a decade or more. In both cases, the distinction between cyclical and "trend" movements in the participation rate and related variables—and in particular, the idea that the trend is independent of the cycle—is not as clear as would be suggested by standard filtering methods.

Three mechanisms for blurring

Among the mechanisms blurring the delineation between the factors that monetary policymakers must accept versus those they can influence are the potential effects of weak aggregate activity on potential labor supply. As many policymakers and analysts have noted and as we discussed in Section 2, the unusual length and severity of the Great Recession, together with the fact that unemployment has been atypically concentrated among the long-term unemployed, seem likely erode the skills and workforce attachment of some unemployed persons. Historically, there has been much less evidence of hysteresis in US labor markets than in European ones, but, as we noted earlier, the severity and unprecedented characteristics of the recent recession suggest the possibility that the United States will not remain free of hysteresis-type effects this time. In principle, hysteresis in labor markets could cause a period of slack demand to have long-lasting adverse implications for the productive capacity of the economy. Accordingly, the ultimate effects of a financial crisis on the potential supply of labor could depend critically on the degree to which monetary policy can limit the initial contraction in real activity, and the speed with which it is able to restore aggregate demand to its normal and sustainable level.

A second channel through which persistent weak aggregate demand could affect aggregate supply involves some aspects of multifactor productivity. Evidence suggests that new-business formation suffers disproportionately during business-cycle downturns, and it is certainly the case that the annual number of start-ups has fallen noticeably since 2007 (upper panel of Figure 3.1). Moreover, employment growth at young firms has also been extremely weak by historical standards over the past few years (lower panel). Haltiwanger et al. (2012) show that young and small businesses were especially hard-hit during the recession and weak recovery, reflecting credit constraints and the steep drop in house prices, which reduced the ability of entrepreneurs to finance startups or expansions with home equity. If start-ups play a disproportionate role in promoting innovation because they embody the latest technologies, then the "demand" factors that have restrained new business formation since the onset of the financial crisis are also probably working to damp growth in multifactor productivity.

Additionally, cyclical changes in research and development (R&D) can have long-lasting effects on multifactor productivity. Simple models generate the prediction that R&D investment will be countercyclical as businesses would be expected to shift resources toward investments with longer-term payoffs when the opportunity costs of allocating resources away from current production is lower. Empirically, however, R&D investment appears to move in a procyclical manner.[28] If so, then recessions likely have a persistent adverse effect on the growth of multifactor productivity. Relatedly, Shleifer (1986) finds that the diffusion of new technologies is slower in recessions than in expansions. In light of this research, and given that real R&D investment has grown only 1.6 percent per year since late 2007, as compared to 3.6 percent on average from 1990 through 2007, it seems reasonable to assume that at least some of the cumulative reduction in trend MFP over the last few years is an endogenous response to weak aggregate demand.

Finally, aggregate demand, and hence monetary policy, can potentially influence the economy's productive potential through its effects on capital deepening. Under the production-function approach to supply-side estimation discussed earlier and employed by the Congressional Budget Office (2001), the International Monetary Fund (2010), the ECB (2010), and many other official institutions, the current level of the capital stock is a key determinant of potential output. Thus, in this accounting framework, the substantial cutback in business outlays on equipment and structures that typically occurs in response to the diminished sales prospects, heightened uncertainty, and tight credit conditions of deep recessions[29] acts not only to reduce current aggregate demand but also to lower the estimated productive capacity of the economy in the future. Although such demand-induced capital deepening effects are presumably not literally

---

[28] See, for example, Diego and Gertler (2006). Barlevy (2007) argues that the procyclicality of R&D reflects externalities that cause firms to undertake more R&D in economic booms than would be optimal. In contrast, Aghion (2012) shows that credit constraints can limit the capacity for firms to invest in R&D during recessions if profits—and thus internal funds—are too low to finance such investments directly.

[29] In theory, the reduced pace of *business* capital deepening in the United States seen since 2007 could be the result of technology shocks that have reduced the marginal return on capital. Arguing against this interpretation, however, is the elevated level of profitability. Alternatively, one might argue that the decline in business investment has been driven at least in part by reduced access to capital associated with permanently tighter underwriting standards and other structural changes in credit markets. Whether the latter phenomenon is best thought of as a technological rather than a demand development is open to debate, however; in any event, the restrictions on credit availability that have emerged since the financial crisis have been more important for households than for businesses (especially large ones). For these reasons, we believe that most of the observed slowdown in business investment is primarily a response to a weak demand environment and heightened uncertainty about the future pace of recovery.

permanent, they are likely to persist for many years given the substantial adjustment costs that characterize business investment.[30]

Some alternative approaches to measuring resource utilization attempt to side-step this issue by estimating potential output using an "equilibrium" concept of the capital stock rather than the actual level. For example, it is common practice in DSGE modeling to define economic slack using a flex-price concept of potential output, in which the latter is computed by simulating how the economy would have evolved over history in the absence of both wage-price frictions and markup shocks. (See Neiss and Nelson, 2003.) This approach yields measures of the equilibrium capital stock and potential output that, at least in theory, are exogenous to the transitory fluctuations in aggregate demand and accompanying changes in monetary policy that occur in the wake of a financial crisis, while allowing the "efficient" effects of changes in tastes and technology on productivity, the composition of output, and other real factors to show through. Thus, policymakers who employ the flex-price concept of potential output arguably have the advantage of seeing through the transitory (albeit drawn out) swings in capital deepening when crafting policy.[31]

While we think it important to distinguish permanent movements in capital from transitory fluctuations, we nonetheless believe that standard flex-price calculations of potential output are problematic. As Woodford (2003) has pointed out, an important rationale for allowing the actual (rather than equilibrium) level of capital services to affect the estimated level of potential output is that firms' marginal costs and productive capacity, and thus aggregate

---

[30] Such drawn-out capital accumulation dynamics are a standard feature of estimated macro models, including the Federal Reserve Board's workhorse FRB/US model and its two DSGE models, EDO and SIGMA.

[31] On the surface, purely statistical methods for extracting trend output, such as the Beveridge-Nelson decomposition or the Hodrick-Prescott filter, might also seem to avoid this issue because they do not condition on any measure of the capital stock. For the reasons discussed earlier, however, such methods have the problem of ascribing to the "trend" any movements in output associated with drawn-out fluctuations in capital services and other inputs, whether or not they are endogenous.

inflation, depend on the actual capital stock, which evolves slowly over a time horizon relevant

for monetary policy. This line of argument suggests to us that central banks should design their

strategies with an eye to both the predicted future path of capital and the effects of their policy

actions on that path (and hence the evolution of potential output, actual employment, and

inflation).[32] Moreover, the standard flex-price calculation ignores the potential for movements in

aggregate demand to influence potential labor input and trend multifactor productivity—effects

that in turn will alter any calculation of the equilibrium capital stock—because these channels are

not accounted for in the standard models used by central banks, DSGE or otherwise. Finally, we

would note that completely delinking the estimated level of potential output from the actual

capital stock, and instead basing it entirely on a theoretical calculation of what the stock would

be in the absence of all nominal frictions and mark-up shocks, suffers from the problem that the

identification of frictions and shocks, and hence the estimated level of potential output, can be

quite sensitive to model specification and assumptions about the nature of shocks—a point

discussed by Kiley (2012).

Quantitative assessment

The foregoing discussion leads to the obvious question: How much of the reduction in

aggregate supply during the past several years has represented an endogenous response to weak

aggregate demand that monetary policy should strive to mitigate, versus an exogenous

development to which monetary policy probably had to acquiesce? Of course it is difficult to

---

[32] Even if an estimate of potential output generated by a DSGE model is based on the actual business capital stock, comparing that estimate to one based on the production-function approach may be problematic because the model's measure of capital may differ noticeably from the official government measure. In part, such differences can arise because DSGE models often define business capital to include residential capital and the stock of consumer durable goods, unlike the non-farm business sector measure used in the state-space analysis discussed earlier. In addition, DSGE models may implicitly use a different methodology for translating the business capital stock into an aggregate flow of capital services. Finally, DSGE models often treat the capital stock as an unobserved variable, an assumption that can result in yet more differences from the official series.

pinpoint the composition of what happened in the past several years, but the state-space model we described earlier suggests that a reduction in capital deepening—which we view as mostly an endogenous response to weak demand—caused almost half of the cumulative shortfall in potential output from its pre-crisis trend. As for the other possible channels, we interpret the available evidence as indicating a modest adverse shift in the basic parameters of the labor market expected to prevail over the longer run; at the same, we stress that it is far too early to rule out the possibility that evidence of more substantial effects may emerge before the economy has fully recovered. And the underlying causes—and likely persistence—of the apparent recent deceleration in trend multifactor productivity are even murkier, although it seems probable that the depressive effects of the recession and reduced credit availability on the rate of new business formation and on R&D expenditures has played some role.

As we noted at the start of this section, our assessment that much of the recent supply-side damage is endogenous has potentially important implications for the conduct of monetary policy. In particular, such damage provides an additional rationale for policymakers to take highly accommodative actions in response to sharp contractions in real activity. In the next section, we illustrate this effect using simulations of a financial crisis under "optimal" policy analysis. In carrying out this analysis, however, we also consider some additional factors that may act to push monetary policy in a less accommodative direction.

IV. Optimal Policy, Endogenous Supply-Side Effects, and Other Considerations

The relevance of the endogeneity discussed in the previous section for monetary (or fiscal) policy relates to the possibility that policymakers may be able craft strategies with an eye to influencing both the supply and the demand sides of the economy. In particular, such policies might differ appreciably from standard strategies that treat the natural rate of unemployment, trend labor force participation, and other components of potential output as if they were exogenous. Along these lines, Adolfson *et al.* (2011) have used simulations of the Riksbank's macro model to show that "optimal" strategies that define potential output using the actual (endogenous) capital stock differ noticeably from ones that define potential GDP using the flex-price equilibrium (and thus policy-invariant) capital stock.

In a similar vein, we conduct simulations using the Federal Reserve workhorse FRB/US macro model that allow for the possibility that a financial crisis and the resulting shortfall in aggregate demand endogenously cause a reduction of potential labor input and capital deepening, along the lines of what seems to have happened during the Great Recession in the United States. Leaving aside some potentially important countervailing considerations, we find that when policymakers recognize the endogeneity of supply-side conditions and optimize accordingly, they adopt a more aggressive approach to the conduct of policy in response to a recession. However, we also emphasize that these other considerations—including concerns that an aggressive policy stance may lead to an increased risk of financial instability or unacceptably high inflation —may appropriately cause policymakers to exercise greater caution.

The FRB/US model

FRB/US is a large-scale model of the economy that has been used extensively by the staff of the Federal Reserve Board since the mid-1990s to study a wide range of monetary and fiscal policy issues. Although FRB/US does not have the tight micro-foundations of a DSGE model, its equations are grounded in the assumption that households and firms are forward-looking and engage in optimization subject to adjustment costs and habit persistence. Roughly 25 percent of consumer spending is estimated to be carried out by rule-of-thumb consumers, while the rest is attributable to life-cycle households who discount the future at a high rate owing to idiosyncratic income risk. The model is very detailed and includes equations for eleven different components of private consumption, investment, exports, and imports; standard asset pricing equations for a variety of long-term interest rates, the stock market, and the exchange rate; a comprehensive accounting of government spending and taxation at both the federal and the state and local levels; and a small-scale foreign sector. Wage and price dynamics are characterized by a new-Keynesian Phillips curve in which marginal costs move with the unemployment gap, defined as the actual unemployment rate less the current value of the natural rate (which, as discussed below, will be augmented to include hysteresis effects).[33]

In the version of FRB/US used in this paper, all financial market participants and agents involved in wage-price setting are assumed to be rational, and monetary policymakers enjoy complete credibility; furthermore, these particular private-sector expectations are assumed to incorporate perfect foresight about the future path of the economy once shocks hit.[34] These expectational assumptions are important for our analysis because the fallout from the illustrative financial crisis that we simulate, in line with the real-world experience of the past few years, is sufficiently severe and protracted to cause short-term interest rates to be constrained by the zero lower bound for several years. As a result, and because for simplicity we leave aside the possibility of large-scale asset purchases, the main tool available to monetary policymakers for stimulating the economy in the near term is to promise to keep the federal funds low in the future, thereby putting downward pressure on long-term interest rates. In the model, this

---

[33] For more information on the FRB/US model, see Brayton and Tinsley (1996), Brayton, Tinsley and Williams (1997), Brayton, Mauskopf, Reifschneider, Tinsley and Williams (1997), and Reifschneider, Tetlow, and Williams (1999).

[34] Other private-sector expectations—most importantly, households' assessments of future income—are generated using a small-scale VAR model; thus, households are forward looking but have only an approximate sense of the dynamics of the economy. Making all private-sector expectations model-consistent (that is, fully rational) would have no qualitative effect on the results reported in this paper but would considerably slow the convergence speed of the optimal-control simulations discussed below, owing to the highly nonlinear nature of the model with the zero lower bound imposed.

pressure in turn reduces the borrowing costs of households and firms, boosts corporate equity prices and other types of household wealth, and promotes net exports through a lower real exchange rate.

Calibration of hysteresis effects

To facilitate the study of endogenous supply-side effects, we modify the standard version of FRB/US (which already includes capital accumulation equations) to also incorporate illustrative hysteresis-like responses of both unemployment and labor force participation to changes in aggregate activity. In particular, we assume that the natural rate of unemployment and the trend labor-force participation rate evolve as follows:

$$U_t^* = .96U_{t-1}^* + .04U^{**} + .02f\left(U_{t-1} - U_{t-1}^*\right)\left[U_{t-1} - U_{t-1}^*\right] + \varepsilon_t$$

$$LFPR_t^* = .96LFPR_{t-1}^* + .04LFPR^{**} - .04f\left(U_{t-1} - U_{t-1}^*\right)\left[U_{t-1} - U_{t-1}^*\right] + \xi_t$$

In these expressions, U^* is the natural rate of unemployment and $LFPR^*$ is the trend rate of labor force participation. Both variables move persistently in response to the unemployment gap ($U-U^*$) and direct shocks (ε and ξ). Nonetheless, both variables also return (very slowly) to their fixed long-run values U^{**} and $LFPR^{**}$.[35] These dynamics are consistent with the idea that, although financial crises and deep recessions can have persistent effects on labor supply by disrupting labor market functioning, impairing unemployed workers' skills, and causing premature permanent departures from the labor force, such events do not alter demographic

---

[35] In the standard version of FRB/US, which incorporates the state-space model discussed in the first section of the paper, the equivalents to U** and LFPR** are subject to permanent shocks; these shocks are idiosyncratic and unrelated to shortfalls in aggregate demand. Such shocks are not relevant for the analysis considered in this section of the paper, however, and so are suppressed here to simplify the analysis.

conditions, the social safety net, or other fundamental determinants of long-run conditions in the labor market.[36]

Because a change in interest rates affects aggregate demand and thus the level of overall employment, monetary policy in the adjusted version of FRB/US can influence potential output not only through the capital accumulation channel but also through the potential supply of labor.[37] Its ability to do so in the model simulations, however, depends importantly on $f(U-U^*)$, a function that indexes the relative strength of the hysteresis effect, and so plays a key role in determining the magnitude of endogenous supply-side effects in the model simulations. As illustrated in Figure 4.1, $f(.)$ is assumed to depend on the unemployment gap in a highly nonlinear manner. Specifically, we assume that the level of resource utilization has no effect on potential labor supply when the unemployment rate is below U^*, but that the marginal effect of labor market slack on the natural rate and trend labor force participation mounts rapidly as U rises above U^*.

This non-linear specification has two important policy implications. First, accommodative monetary policy can limit the amount of endogenous damage to labor supply if it can limit the amount of time the unemployment gap is above about 1¼ percent (the value of the unemployment rate gap above which f() becomes substantial). Although this specification is *ad hoc*, and in particular the threshold of 1¼ percent is somewhat arbitrarily chosen, such "threshold" behavior in general seems consistent with the observation that warning signals that figure prominently in today's landscape, such as a marked increase in long-duration unemployment and a persistent fall in labor force participation, were largely missing in the

---

[36] The Scandinavian labor markets do appear to have changed permanently after their financial crisis, but these long-run changes plausibly reflected legislative changes to labor laws and other aspects of the social safety net.
[37] In contrast, we assume that the FRB/US simulations do not provide any mechanism for activist monetary policy to offset the adverse supply-side effects of direct shocks to U^* or $LFPR^*$.

milder recessions seen earlier in the post-World-War-II period in the United States. A second important implication of this specification is that policymakers cannot undo labor market damage once it has occurred, but must instead wait for it to fade away on its own accord; in other words, there is no special advantage, given this specification, to running a high-pressure economy along the lines suggested by Okun (1973).[38] Such quasi-irreversibility seems consistent with both the tendency for older workers who leave the labor force prematurely on account of unemployment to never return and the persistent stigma experienced by the long-term unemployed.

Simulated effects of an illustrative financial crisis

Using the modified FRB/US model, we now develop an illustrative scenario involving a major financial crisis that has persistent effects on both aggregate demand and aggregate supply; by design, the macroeconomic effects of this shock are broadly similar to those seen to date since 2007. In this scenario, the economy is hit with a disruption to financial markets that causes a sharp contraction in household spending, business investment, and employment in response to higher risk premiums on a range of financial assets, falling house prices, and direct shocks to spending and hiring similar to those experienced during the financial crisis and subsequent deep recession.[39] In addition, the economy experiences exogenous disruptions to productivity and

---

[38] The specification of $f(U-U^*)$ as well as the coefficients of the two equations have been calibrated to yield endogenous movements in U^* and $LFPR^*$ that, in the context of the financial crisis scenario discussed below, appear roughly consistent with the experience of the last few years. Arguably, it would have been better to estimate these equations (and the shape of the scaling function) rather than calibrate them. However, given the lack of historical evidence for hysteresis effects in the United States prior to the current episode, and given that our simulations are intended to explore the *possible* implications of recent events (as opposed to the most likely ones), we doubt that results from any time-series exercise would be particularly illuminating.

[39] These direct shocks are presumed to reflect those effects of a financial crisis that operate through channels not formally accounted for in the model's structure, such as a reduced access to credit as a result of tighter lending standards and persistent balance-sheet problems, increased uncertainty about future household income and corporate earnings, and a general deterioration in consumer and business confidence. In the context of many DSGE models (including the Fed's EDO model), the effects of such disruptions are typically captured through an economy-wide risk premium shock intended to provide a theoretical explanation for the correlated downturn in consumption and investment. Nevertheless, like FRB/US, current DSGE models do not really provide a satisfactory accounting of the various linkages between financial markets and the real economy that come into play during a financial crisis.

labor market functioning (resulting in a rise in the natural rate) in addition to those that arise endogenously in response to weak aggregate demand (which adversely affect both the natural rate and trend labor force participation). Finally, the effects of all these adverse events are exacerbated by zero-lower-bound (ZLB) restrictions on the ability of monetary policymakers to counteract the weakness in aggregate demand, and by the failure of the fiscal authorities to initiate any discretionary countercyclical policy response.

Results (expressed as deviations from a steady-state baseline) for this scenario under an inertial policy rule[40] are summarized in Figure 4.2.[41] As can be seen in the upper left panel, the illustrative financial crisis and its restraining effect on aggregate demand cause the output gap to widen more than 6 percentage points after two years and inflation to fall more than 1½ percentage points relative to baseline. In response, the inertial policy rule causes the federal funds rate to drop 450 basis points over the first two years, after which no further reduction is possible because of the ZLB. Nevertheless, by adhering to an inertial rather than non-inertial rule, policymakers are able to provide greater stimulus to near-term activity because the inertial rule takes a gradualist approach to returning the funds rate to a normal level after the ZLB no longer binds, thereby reducing bond yields and improving financial conditions more generally.[42] Economic conditions gradually begin to improve starting in the third year, although the pace of

[40] Specifically, the rule is $R(t) = .85\ R(t-1) + .15\ \{2 + PI(t) + 0.5\ [PI(t) - 2] + 1.0\ Y(t)\}$, where R is the nominal funds rate, PI is the four-quarter rate of core PCE inflation, and Y is the output gap. A non-inertial version of this rule is discussed in Taylor (1999).

[41] In the baseline, the unemployment rate, inflation, and the nominal federal funds rate are constant at 5.5 percent, 2 percent, and 4.5 percent, respectively. The results reported in this section are largely insensitive to these baseline assumptions, with the critical exception of nominal interest rates. Because the simulations incorporate the zero lower bound constraint, the baseline setting of the federal funds rate has an important bearing on the ability of monetary policy to offset the financial crisis.

[42] For simplicity, in this simulation and the others that follow we ignore the possibility that policymakers could use large-scale asset purchases to mitigate the constraint imposed by the zero lower bound.

recovery is painfully slow—a profile similar in many respects to the actual experience of the U.S. economy since the recession ended in mid-2009.

As shown in the upper-right panel, the scenario—like the actual economy in recent years, according to our state-space results—features a noticeable deterioration in the economy's productive capacity, with potential GDP more than 4 percent below its baseline level by the fifth year of the simulation. Most of this decline represents an endogenous response to the persistently weak state of aggregate demand: Just over 40 percent of it is attributable to less capital deepening as a result of a lower level of business investment, while a slightly smaller portion is attributable to hysteresis effects that add almost ½ percentage point to the natural rate and reduce the trend labor force participation rate by a full percentage point (shown in the bottom two panels). However, not all the damage is endogenous: About 20 percent of the reduction in potential GDP reflects the combined influence of an exogenous drop in trend multifactor productivity and a ¼ percentage point rise in the natural rate caused by direct shocks to the U^* equation. As can be seen, this supply-side damage—both endogenous and exogenous—takes years to fade away, and is still noticeably depressing actual output and employment more than a decade after the initial crisis.

"Optimal" policy responses

While the inertial policy rule prescribes a fairly aggressive response to the financial crisis, it nevertheless does not prevent unemployment from rising sharply and remaining elevated for years; nor does it prevent inflation from remaining persistently well below target. Policymakers who recognize the likely magnitude and persistence of the crisis at the onset would obviously be interested in policies that would deliver better outcomes. As discussed by Svensson (2003 and 2005), one standard approach to this problem is to use optimal control techniques. Under this approach, policymakers first specify a loss function that reflects their preferences regarding outcomes for employment, inflation, and other conditions. They then solve for the path of the funds rate that minimizes the loss function, conditional on the dynamics of the economy (as approximated by some model) and the expected evolution of the underlying shocks to the economy.[43]

Optimal-control solutions are, not surprisingly, sensitive to the specification of policymakers' preferences as reflected in the loss function, as well as the specification of the way that they perceive the economy as operating. First, the "optimal" policy response to a crisis will depend not only on the extent of supply-side damage that policymakers expect, but also on whether they believe that damage can be mitigated by their own actions. Second, the optimal policy response will be sensitive to the desired objectives of policy. If an economic slump has resulted in a persistently higher natural rate of unemployment, lower labor force participation, and less capital accumulation, then a policymaker who aims to close the unemployment gap will acquiesce in a greater loss in employment and output than could be achieved with a more aggressive response (for example, by aiming to restore the employment-to-population ratio to its pre-recession trajectory).

We illustrate these sensitivities by displaying outcomes that are derived under alternative assumptions regarding the policymaker's perceptions of the dynamics of the economy including the likely implications of the financial crisis for the supply side of the economy, holding the specification of the loss function constant. In our baseline specification of the loss function—which conforms in spirit with the FOMC's dual mandate—policymakers at time *t0* (the onset of

---

[43] See Svensson and Tetlow (2005) for an illustration of this technique using the FRB/US model and a discussion of its use in FOMC briefing documents. Also see Yellen (2012) for an illustration of its application to the current economic situation.

the financial crisis) wish to find the path for the federal funds rate R over the next M quarters that would be expected to minimize a quadratic loss function L that penalizes (a) squared deviations of unemployment from the conventionally-measured natural rate; (b) squared deviations of inflation from the policymaker's 2 percent goal; and (c) squared changes in the policy rate, as follows:[44]

$$L_{t0} = E_{t0} \sum_{j=0}^{N} \beta^j \left\{ \alpha_1 \left(U_{t0+j} - U^*_{t0+j} \right)^2 + \alpha_2 \left(\pi_{t0+j} - 2 \right)^2 + \alpha_3 \left(\Delta R_{t0+j} \right)^2 \right\}.$$

In our optimal-control analysis, M (the number of quarters in the optimized path of R) is always set to 100 quarters while N (the number of quarters over which the loss function is evaluated) is set to 160 quarters; in addition, the discount factor β is set to .99 and the three α loss weights are all set to unity.[45] Beyond quarter $t0+M$, when the optimized path ends, the federal funds rate is assumed to follow the prescriptions of the inertial policy rule.[46]

Using this baseline loss function, we allow the policymaker to choose the optimal path of the funds rate subject to different beliefs about the nature of the economy and the effects of the financial crisis. These contrasting beliefs are bookended on one side by a poorly-informed view that is mostly oblivious to the adverse implications of a deep recession for supply-side conditions, and on the other side by a view that is based on a full understanding of supply-side

---

[44] In addition to aiming to keep unemployment near its natural rate and inflation near the FOMC's 2 percent target, the loss function penalizes quarter-to-quarter movements in the federal funds rate. In reality, such movements would be destabilizing and thus would have adverse effects on financial markets and the broader economy, implying that such movements would be avoided in optimal-control simulations because of their effects on the unemployment gap. However, the FRB/US model does not incorporate any mechanism for such volatility to affect financial conditions and real activity through risk premiums or some other channel, so the third term is added to the loss function to prevent unrealistically large quarterly movements in short-term interest rates in the optimal-control simulations.

[45] Increasing the value of either M or N has essentially no effect on our simulation results, as does modestly changing the discount factor or altering the relative loss weights (say, by increasing one of them to 5).

[46] Optimal-control strategies of this sort raise issues of time consistency and how policy should be reoptimized in light of previous commitments and incoming data surprises. These questions are beyond the scope of this paper, however, and in the simulations discussed below we assume that policymakers do not re-optimize the trajectory for the path of the funds rate beyond $t0$.

dynamics—a progression that helps to illuminate the implications of different supply-side considerations for optimal policy and associated macroeconomic outcomes. Specifically, we consider three cases:

- In the first case, policymakers fail to recognize the damage to potential labor input and trend multifactor productivity, both endogenous and exogenous, that will occur in the wake of the crisis, as well as policy's potential ability to mitigate that damage. (The one aspect of the damage to the supply side that they correctly anticipate is the reduction in business capital and hence capital deepening.) Accordingly, policymakers view the outcomes reported in Figure 4.2 as too pessimistic because they incorrectly forecast the natural rate, trend labor force participation, and trend multifactor productivity to follow the paths projected before the crisis.[47]

- In the second case, policymakers do understand that financial crises adversely affect the supply side of the economy, so they correctly project that the economy will evolve as shown in Figure 4.2 if monetary policy follows the prescriptions of the inertial policy rule. Policymakers err, however, in failing to recognize that some of this projected supply-side damage could be averted under a more aggressively countercyclical monetary policy; that is, in optimizing the path of the federal funds rate they mistakenly treat the projections of the natural rate and trend labor force participation shown in Figure 4.2 as exogenous.

- In the third case, policymakers correctly understand both the underlying outlook for the economy as illustrated in Figure 4.2 and the "true" dynamics of the economy as captured by

---

[47] Although movements in trend labor force participation and trend multifactor productivity do not figure *directly* in the loss function, their recognition (or lack thereof) by policymakers matters to any computation of optimal monetary policy because changes in these supply-side factors alter policymaker forecasts of potential output, permanent household income, and expected future profits, and hence aggregate demand, employment, and the unemployment rate.

the hysteresis-modified FRB/US model. Only in this case, then, is optimal policy computed based on a fully correct understanding of both the underlying mechanics of the economy and the ability of monetary policy to influence those mechanics.

In the first two cases, policymakers compute an "optimal" path of the federal funds that is based on incorrect information—that is, the wrong model and/or underlying forecast. However, if the funds rate were to follow this path the economy would not evolve as expected by policymakers. We assume that the central bank responds to the unexpected movements in output and inflation by deviating from the originally-planned funds rate path by the amount prescribed by the inertial rule.[48]

The results from this exercise for resource utilization, inflation, and other indicators of demand-side conditions are plotted in Figure 4.3. Among the three cases, the most accommodative *planned* response is chosen by policymakers who neither fully anticipate the supply-side fallout from the financial crisis nor recognize the feedback of their actions on potential labor supply (the blue dashed lines in the upper-left panel), while the least accommodative *planned* response is undertaken by policymakers who anticipate the supply-side damage but fail to recognize their ability to mitigate it (the red dashed lines). Policymakers who fully understand the mechanics of the economy, including their own role in influencing it through feedback effects, chart a middle course (the green solid line).

---

[48] Alternatively put, policymakers implement the two misinformed optimal strategies by first computing what quarter-by-quarter adjustments (or add-factors) to the inertial rule would be necessary to replicate the optimal funds rate path conditional on their initial expectations for the future evolution of the output gap and inflation; then, as events actually unfold, they follow the prescriptions of the inertial rule *plus* the add factors that were computed at *t0*. For simplicity, after time t0 policymakers' estimates of the output gap used in the adjusted inertial policy rule are assumed to reflect the true level of potential output, including hysteresis effects. Implementing the well-informed optimal strategy in the same manner would yield the originally-planned path for the funds rate and associated predicted outcomes, as output and inflation evolve as originally predicted, implying no need to adjust the funds rate over time using the adjusted inertial policy rule.

Actual outcomes for both output and the unemployment rate under the misinformed optimal strategies (the solid blue and red lines) turn out to be close to those achieved under the fully-informed plan (the green solid line) for the first eight years or so, reflecting adjustments to the originally-planned funds rate paths that are undertaken in response to what policymakers see as unexpected movements in output and inflation. A different result obtains with respect to inflation, primarily because inflation in the first decade depends not only on average degree of slack over that period but also on resource utilization further off into the future. Specifically, when policymakers ignore supply-side developments altogether in crafting an optimal response to the crisis, actual inflation runs persistently above that achieved under the full-information strategy, and thus this strategy can be regarded as inappropriately loose in hindsight. Conversely, when policymakers are somewhat better informed but still fail to recognize their ability to mitigate hysteresis effects, actual inflation runs persistently below the full-information strategy, and so policy turns out to be inappropriately tight.

Figure 4.4 compares the (actual) supply-side effects of the financial crisis under these various optimal policies relative to what occurs under the inertial policy rule. As can be seen, because all three "optimal" strategies provide more stimulus to aggregate demand, all result in significantly less damage to the labor market and capital deepening. As a result, the peak decline in potential GDP relative to baseline is roughly cut in half, with the largest improvement occurring under full-information optimal policy, and the smallest under the strategy that anticipates the supply-side damage but fails to take account of policy's ability to mitigate it. That said, the differences in supply-side outcomes across the three "optimal" strategies are relatively minor.

To this point, the policymaker in our simulations has not cared directly about the behavior of the natural rate or trend labor force participation, only about the conventionally-measured unemployment gap and the deviation of inflation from the 2 percent target. Intuitively, optimal policy should become even more accommodative if the central bank did not target the unemployment gap but instead aimed at keeping the employment-to-population ratio near the trend level that would prevail in the absence of hysteresis effects and exogenous (but ultimately transitory) shocks to the natural rate.[49] This intuition is correct, as shown by the magenta lines in Figures 4.3 and 4.4. As can be seen, this strategy holds the nominal federal funds rate at zero appreciably longer than what occurs under U-U^* targeting. (The differences are more noticeable for the *real* federal funds rate because inflation is higher.) This strategy results in persistently lower unemployment and higher real GDP, which in part reflects the effectiveness of the strategy in mitigating hysteresis effects in the labor market, increasing capital deepening, and boosting potential output. And although the strategy also results in inflation noticeably above the 2-percent target for several years, that additional inflation is worthwhile from the perspective of policymakers, both because it mitigates the effects of the ZLB and so helps to boost real activity through lower real interest rates, and because it keeps inflation close to the 2 percent target during the early years of the simulation.

Offsetting considerations and other caveats

By themselves, the simulation results presented in Figures 4.3 and 4.4 would seem to suggest that monetary policymakers should consider adopting more-aggressive responses to deep recessions than would be suggested by standard policy rules in order to mitigate endogenous

---

[49] Alternatively, policymakers could aim to target a trend employment-to-population ratio that incorporated the effects of hysteresis. However, this strategy yields results that are quite similar to that obtained under the baseline specification of the loss function.

supply-side effects. This conclusion, however, overlooks the fact that policymakers may have countervailing concerns that are not accounted for in the optimal-control exercises. In particular, policymakers may be worried that pursuing a highly accommodative monetary policy for a long time could inadvertently sow the seeds for a future financial crisis. Such a development might occur if persistently low short-term interest rates were to prompt firms to take on increasing amounts of leverage—thereby decreasing the stability of the financial system—or prompt investors to take on an inappropriate amount of risk in a reach for yield. In light of these risks, policymakers might appropriately opt for a more conservative response to a major economic downturn, even if they recognized the potential adverse effects on the supply side of the economy.

To illustrate this possibility, we compute optimal policy responses to a major financial crisis in a scenario in which persistently low short-term interest rates would eventually result in a second financial crisis. In this exercise, the magnitude of the original financial shock is the same as before and is accompanied by the same endogenous supply-side effects. However, policymakers now confront an unpleasant trade-off: The more they attempt to stimulate aggregate demand by promising to keep current and future short-term rates at a low level, the greater is the magnitude of a second financial crisis, which is assumed to occur, for sure, in the tenth year of the scenario. Specifically, the longer and the lower they hold the nominal federal funds rate below 1½ percent over the nine years following the onset of the initial financial crisis, the larger are the shocks that hit the economy in the tenth year. For simplicity, these second-round shocks are re-scaled versions of those that occurred during the first crisis, where the scaling factor is

$$\Omega = \mu \sum_{t=1}^{36} d_t \left(1.5 - R_t\right),$$

with $d_t = 1$ if $R_t < 1.5$, 0 otherwise. (An implication of this specification is that the policymakers cannot offset the destabilizing financial effects of very low interest rates by pushing them to unusually high levels later.) The parameter μ is calibrated so that the deterioration in real activity following the second crisis is about the same as in the first if policymakers follow the prescriptions of the inertial policy rule throughout.

Results from this exercise are reported in Figure 4.5 for three optimal-control policies. The first repeats the results from Figures 4.3 and 4.4, for the case in which policymakers strive to keep the employment-to-population ratio near its time-invariant long-run equilibrium level (i.e., *E**/P*) and inflation near 2 percent while trying to avoid large quarter-to-quarter movements in the federal funds rate, without any consideration of financial-stability effects. In the second set of results (the green lines), policymakers elect to avoid a second crisis altogether by optimizing subject to the constraint that the federal funds rate is never allowed to fall below 1½ percent. By contrast, in the third case (the red lines), they actively trade off the benefits of a more-aggressive policy now, with its attendant reduction of supply-side damage, against the costs of a more-severe financial crisis in the future. Given the specific parameterization implemented here, policymaker loss is minimized with a future financial crisis that is 40 percent smaller than the immediate one, but near-term supply-side damage is less than when they pursue a less accommodative strategy that avoids a second financial crisis altogether. In both the second and third cases, optimal monetary policy is noticeably more restrictive on average over the first nine years than in the situation where very accommodative monetary policy does not have adverse effects on financial stability (magenta lines).

The willingness of policymakers to pursue an aggressive monetary response to a recession should also depend on their views about the likely efficacy of their policy actions.

That is, policymakers should be engaged in a cost-benefit calculation that balances, on the one hand, the expected macroeconomic benefits from greater monetary accommodation and hence stronger aggregate demand and diminished supply-side effects, and on the other hand, the expected losses from sparking a future crisis. The more effective that a marginal easing in the stance of monetary policy is in moving employment and inflation, the more that policymakers should engage in such easing—even if there are collateral costs in terms of reduced financial stability. And, of course, the converse statement holds.

Threats to financial stability are not the only offsetting concern that might limit policymakers' willingness to fight endogenous supply-side damage; for example, they may also be reluctant to implement a highly accommodative strategy because of concerns about its potential adverse effects on inflation expectations and inflation dynamics more generally. In the optimal-control analysis presented in this paper, wage and price expectations are rational, policymakers enjoy complete credibility, and the parameters of the new Keynesian inflation process are stable and invariant to changes in monetary policy—assumptions that almost certainly do not hold in reality. And even though Kiley (2007), Laforte (2007), and others have found that empirical new Keynesian inflation models of the sort used in FRB/US and in DSGE models do provide a reasonable approximation to the observed behavior of inflation over the past twenty years or so, policymakers might well worry that inflation dynamics could evolve in a highly undesirable and costly direction if monetary policy were to depart markedly from recent historical norms, perhaps even returning to the instability seen during the 1970s.

Finally, we should stress that the optimal-control exercises that we have conducted here ignore policymaker uncertainty, which is ubiquitous in the real world.[50] In the wake of a financial crisis, real-world policymakers cannot be sure about the extent of supply-side damage that has occurred even well after the fact, let alone the proportion that reflects an endogenous response to weak aggregate demand. In addition, they cannot be sure about the ability of a more-accommodative policy stance to check the initial damage that occurs or to subsequently repair it, particularly in an environment in which the ability of monetary policy to influence aggregate demand may be impaired. Finally, the effects of persistently accommodative monetary policy on financial stability and the stability of inflation expectations are also highly uncertain. How policymakers should respond to such pervasive uncertainty is not obvious, especially if they (or the private agents on whose behalf they act) are not risk-neutral. On the one hand, Brainard-type considerations might argue for taking a more cautious approach to trying to head off supply-side damage than suggested by the optimal-control simulations shown earlier, given uncertainty about the effectiveness of monetary policy in mitigating supply-side damage. On the other hand, a robust control approach might call for a more aggressive response if the adverse tail event of primary concern involved endogenous supply-side damage.[51] In any event, uncertainty about both the extent and nature of supply-side damage, as well as about the possible side effects of a persistently accommodative stance of policy, greatly complicates the decision-making process

---

[50] As is well known, uncertainty has little or no role to play in optimal decisionmaking when preferences are well described by a quadratic loss function and the economy is linear. (In our analysis, we have sidestepped the fact that the FRB/US model is not strictly linear, especially in the presence of the zero lower bound.) In reality, however, the actual economy sometimes experiences highly non-linear dynamics; moreover, policymakers' concerns are not adequately captured by a simple loss function. For these and other reasons, uncertainty assuredly plays an important role in policymaker deliberations in the real world.

[51] Of course, if policymakers were instead concerned about minimizing the risk of a future financial crisis, then robust control might argue for a less activist strategy.

because it forces policymakers to weigh the costs and probabilities associated with a range of risks and possible outcomes.

Conclusions

This paper has reviewed the evidence for supply-side damage in the wake of the financial crisis and considered some of its implications for monetary policy. In the labor market, matching efficiency seems to have been somewhat impaired, the natural rate of unemployment appears to have risen somewhat, and trend labor force participation appears to have moved noticeably lower relative to what would have been expected based on pre-crisis trends. In addition, the capital stock and trend multifactor productivity are appreciably lower than what would have been predicted in 2007. Our point estimates suggest that, in combination, these developments—whose eventual magnitude was arguably apparent only in hindsight—shaved almost 7 percent off the level of potential output relative to its pre-crisis trend. That said, the uncertainty about this estimate is extremely high and the implications for future growth are quite uncertain.

Despite this supply-side damage, our point estimates also suggest that the level of economic slack has been and remains substantial. As has been noted by a number of observers, this factor by itself would argue for a highly accommodative monetary policy, particularly in an environment of what appears to be quite well-anchored inflation expectations. We have argued that the case for aggressive policy is strengthened further by the likelihood that much of the supply-side damage is an endogenous response to weak aggregate demand. As our simulation analysis illustrates, optimal monetary policy becomes noticeably more accommodative in the wake of a major financial crisis if the natural rate of unemployment and trend labor force participation are subject to hysteresis-like effects that policy might be able to mitigate.

However, we have also argued that policymakers may adopt a more restrained response to a deep recession if they fear the attendant risks to financial stability, or are concerned that inflation expectations may become unanchored. More generally, the pervasive uncertainty in which policymakers operate may encourage them to proceed with caution.

References

Aaronson, Daniel, Jonathan Davis, and Luojia Hu (2012). "Explaining the Decline in the U.S. Labor Force Participation Rate," *Chicago Fed Letter*, No. 13.

Aaronson, Stephanie, Bruce Fallick, Andrew Figura, Jonathan Pingle, and William Wascher (2006). "The Recent Decline in the Labor Force Participation Rate and Its Implications for Potential Labor Supply," *Brookings Papers on Economic Activity*, no. 1, pp.69-154.

Abraham, Katherine G. and Lawrence F. Katz (1986). "Cyclical Unemployment: Sectoral Shifts or Aggregate Disturbances?" *Journal of Political Economy*, 94(3): 507-522.

Adolfson, Malin, Stefan Laseen, Jesper Linde, and Lars E. O. Svensson (2011). "Optimal Monetary Policy in an Operational Medium-Sized DSGE Model," Journal of Money, Credit, and Banking, 43(7), 1287-1331.

Aghion, Philippe, Philippe Askenazy, Nicolas Berman, Gilbert Cette, and Laurent Eymard (2012). "Credit Constraints and the Cyclicality of R&D Investment: Evidence from France," *Journal of the European Economic Association,* 10(5): 1001-1024.

Akerlof, George A., William T. Dickens, and George L. Perry (1996). "The Macroeconomics of Low Inflation," *Brookings Papers on Economic Activity*, no. 1, pp.1-75.

Ascari, Guido and Argia M. Sbordone (2013). "The Macroeconomics of Trend Inflation," *Federal Reserve Bank of New York Staff Reports* No. 628 (August).

Autor, David and Mark Duggan (2006). "The Growth in the Social Security Disability Rolls: A Fiscal Crisis Unfolding," *Journal of Economic Perspectives*, 20(3): 71-96.

Baily, Martin, James Manyika, and Shalabh Gupta (2013). "U.S. Productivity Growth: An Optimistic Perspective," *International Productivity Monitor*, No. 25(1):3-12.

Ball, Laurence (1999). "Aggregate Demand and Long-Run Unemployment," *Brookings Papers on Economic Activity*, 2, 189-251.

Ball, Laurence, Daniel Leigh and Prakash Loungani (2013). "Okun's Law: Fit at 50?" NBER Working Paper 18668.

Barlevy, Gadi (2007). "On the Cyclicality of Research and Development," *American Economic Review*, 97(4): 1131-1164.

Barnichon, Regis and Andrew Figura (2013). "Labor Market Heterogeneities and the Aggregate Matching Function," unpublished manuscript, September 2013.

Barro, Robert J. and David B. Gordon (1983). "A Positive Theory of Monetary Policy in a Natural-Rate Model," *Journal of Political Economy*, 91(4): 589-610.

Basistha, Arabinda and Richard Startz (2008). "Measuring the NAIRU with Reduced Uncertainty: A Muliple-Indicator Common-Cycle Approach," *Review of Economics and Statistics* 90, 805-811.

Basu, Susanto and John G. Fernald (2009). "What Do We Know (and Not Know) About Potential Output?" *Federal Reserve Bank of St. Louis Review* (July), 187-214.

Beveridge, S. and C. R. Nelson (1981). "A New Approach to the Decomposition of Economic Time Series Into Permanent and Transitory Components with Particular Attention to Measurement of the Business Cycle," *Journal of Monetary Economics* 7(x): 151-174.

Blanchard, Olivier J. and Lawrence H. Summers (1986). "Hysteresis and the European Unemployment Problem," *NBER Macroeconomics Annual*, 1, 15-90.

Blanchard, Olivier J. and Danny Quah (1989). "The Dynamic Effects of Aggregate Demand and Supply Disturbances," *American Economic Review* 79, 655-673.

Blanchard, Olivier J. (2003). "Monetary Policy and Unemployment," remarks at *Monetary Policy and the Labor Market: A Conference in Honor of James Tobin*, New School, New York, November 2002.

Borio, Claudio, Piti Disyatat and Mikael Juselius (2013). "Rethinking Potential Output: Embedding Information about the Financial Cycle," *Bank of International Settlements Working Papers* No. 404.

Brayton, Flint and Peter Tinsley, eds. (1996). "A Guide to FRB/US—A Macroeconomic Model of the United States," Federal Reserve Board *Finance and Economics Discussion Series Paper* No. 1996-42.

Brayton, Flint, Andrew T. Levin, Ralph Tryon, and John C. Williams (1997). "The Evolution of Macro Models at the Federal Reserve Board," *Carnegie-Rochester Conference Series on Public Policy* 47, 227-245.

Brayton, Flint, Eileen Mauskopf, David Reifschneider, Peter Tinsley, and John C. Williams (1997). "The Role of Expectations in the FRB/US Macroeconomic Model," *Federal Reserve Bulletin* 83 (April), 43-81.

Brynjolfsson, Erik and Andrew McAfee (2011). *Race Against the Machine: How the Digital Revolution of Accelerating Innovation, Driving Productivity, and Irreversibly Transforming Employment and the Economy*. Digital Frontier Press.

Byrne, David M., Steven D. Oliner, and Daniel E. Sichel (2013). "Is the Information Technology Revolution Over?" *International Productivity Monitor*, 25(1): 20-36.

Cerra, Valerie and Sweta Chaman Saxena (2008). "Growth Dynamics: The Myth of Economic Recovery," *American Economic Review*, 98(1): 439-57.

Chung, Hess, Michael Kiley, and Jean-Philippe Laforte (2012). "Unemployment During the Great Recession in the EDO Model of the U.S. Economy: The 2012 EDO Model." Federal Reserve Board Finance and Economics Discussion Paper No.

Clark, Peter K. (1987). "The Cyclical Component of U.S. Economic Activity," *Quarterly Journal of Economics* 102(4): 797-814.

Clark, Todd (2011). "Real-Time Density Forecasts from Bayesian Vector Autoregressions with Stochastic Volatility," *Journal of Business and Economic Statistics*, 29, 327-341.

Comin, Diego and Mark Gertler (2006). "Medium-Term Business Cycles," American Economic Review, 96(3): 523-551.

Congressional Budget Office (2001). "CBO's Method for Estimating Potential Output: An Update," Congress of the United States, Washington, D.C. (August).

Congressional Budget Office (2012). "What Accounts for the Slow Growth of the Economy After the Recession?" Congress of the United States, Washington, D.C. (November).

Daly, Mary C., Bart Hobijn, Aysegul Sahin, and Rob Valletta (2012). "A Search and Matching Approach to Labor Markets: Did the Natural Rate of Unemployment Rise?" *Journal of Economic Perspectives*, 26(3): 3-26.

Daly, Mary C., and Bart Hobijn (2013). "Downward Nominal Wage Rigidities Bend the Phillips Curve," *Federal Reserve Bank of San Francisco Working Paper No. 2013-08*.

Davis, Steven J., Jason Faberman and John C. Haltiwanger (2012). "Recruiting Intensity During and After the Great Recession: National and Industry Evidence," *American Economic Review*, 102(3):, 584-88.

Del Negro, Marco, Marc P. Giannoni, and Frank Schorfheide (2013). "Inflation in the Great Recession and New Keynesian Models," *Federal Reserve Bank of New York Staff Reports* No. 618 (May).

Delong, J. Bradford, and Lawrence H. Summers (2012). "Fiscal Policy in a Depressed Economy," *Brookings Papers on Economic Activity*, Spring, 233-297.

De Masi, P. (1997). "IMF Estimates of Potential Output: Theory and Practice," *Staff Studies for the World Economic Outlook*, December.

Diamond, Peter (2013). "Cyclical Unemployment, Structural Unemployment," *Federal Reserve Bank of Boston Working Paper* No. 13-5.

Dornbush, Rudiger, and Stanley Fischer (1978). *Macroeconomics*, McGraw-Hill.

Erceg, Christopher J. and Andrew T. Levin (2013). "Labor Force Participation and Monetary Policy in the Wake of the Great Recession," working paper (IMF).

European Central Bank (2000). "Potential Output and Output Gaps," *ECB Monthly Bulletin*, October 2000: 37-48.

European Central Bank (2011). "Trends in Potential Output," *ECB Monthly Bulletin*, January 2011, 73-85.

Farber, Henry S. and Robert G. Valletta (2013). "Do Extended Unemployment Benefits Lengthen Unemployment Spells? Evidence from Recent Cycles in the U.S. Labor Market," *Federal Reserve Bank of San Francisco Working Paper Series* No. 2013-09.

Fernald, John G. (2012). "Productivity and Potential Output Before, During and After the Great Recession," Federal Reserve Bank of San Francisco Working Paper 2012-18.

Figura, Andrew, and William Wascher (2010). "The Causes and Consequences of Sectoral Reallocation: Evidence from the Early 21st Century," *Business Economics*, 45(1): pp.49-68.

Fleischman, Charles A. and John M. Roberts (2011). "From Many Series, One Cycle: Improved Estimates of the Business Cycle from a Multivariate Unobserved Components Model," Federal Reserve Board *Finance and Economics Discussion Series* No. 2011-46.

Fort, Teresa, John Haltiwanger, Ron S. Jarmin, and Javier Miranda (2013). "How Firms Respond to Business Cycles: The Role of the Firm Age and Firm Size," *NBER Working Paper* No. 19134.

Gordon, Robert J. (2003). "Exploding Productivity Growth: Context, Causes, and Implications," *Brookings Papers on Economic Activity*, 2003, 2, 207-79.

Gordon, Robert J. (2012). "Is U.S. Economic Growth Over? Faltering Innovation Confronts the Six Headwinds," *NBER Working Paper* No. 18315.

Gordon, Robert J. (2013). "U.S. Productivity Growth: The Slowdown Has Returned After a Temporary Revival," *International Productivity Monitor*, No. 25(1):13-19.

Haltmaier, Jane. (2012). "Do Recessions Affect Potential Output?" Federal Reserve Board *International Finance Discussion Paper* No. 1066 (December).

Hassett, Kevin A. (2013). "A Long-Term Problem for the Economy," *National Review* (May 10).

Hornstein, Andreas (2013). "The Cyclicality of the Labor Force Participation Rate," Working Paper, Federal Reserve Bank of Richmond.

Kiley, Michael T. (2007). "A Quantitative Comparison of Sticky-Price and Sticky-Information Models of Price Setting," Journal of Money, Credit, and Banking, 39(S1): 101-125.

Kiley, Michael T. (2012). "Output Gaps," Federal Reserve Board *Finance and Economic Discussion Series* 2010-27.

Kroft, Kory, Fabian Lange, and Matthew J. Notowidigdo (2013). "Duration Dependence and Labor Market Conditions: Evidence from a Field Experiment," *Quarterly Journal of Economics*, 128(3): 1123-1167.

Kuttner, Kenneth N. (1994). "Estimating Potential Output as a Latent Variable," *Journal of Business and Economic Statistics* 12, 361-368.

Kuttner, Kenneth N. and Adam S. Posen (2001). "The Great Recession: Lessons for Macroeconomic Policy from Japan," *Brookings Papers on Economic Activity*, 2, 93-160.

Laforte, Jean-Philippe (2007). "Pricing Models: A Bayesian DSGE Approach for the U.S. Economy," *Journal of Money, Credit, and Banking*, 39(s1), 127-154.

Lazear, Edward P. and James R. Spletzer (2012). "The United States Labor Market: Status Quo or a New Normal?"in *The Changing Policy Landscape*, Federal Reserve Bank of Kansas City Economic Policy Symposium, 405-451.

Lilien, David M. (1982), "Sectoral Shifts and Cyclical Unemployment," *Journal of Political Economy* 90 (August): 777-93.

Loungani, Prakesh, and Richard Rogerson (1989). "Cyclical Fluctuations and the Sectoral Reallocation of Labor: Evidence from the PSID," *Journal of Monetary Economics*, 23(2): 259-273.

Lucas, Robert E. Jr. (1971). "Econometric Testing of the Natural Rate Hypothesis," *The Econometrics of Price Determination*, Board of Governors of the Federal Reserve System.

Martin, Robert, and Beth Anne Wilson (2013) "Potential Output and Recessions: Are We Fooling Ourselves," unpublished working paper, Federal Reserve Board.

Molloy, Raven Saks, Christopher L. Smith and Abigail Wozniak (2013). "Internal Migration in the United States," *Journal of Economic Perspectives* 25(3): 173-196.

Mueller, Andreas I., Jesse Rothstein, and Till M. von Wachter (2013). "Unemployment Insurance and Disability Insurance in the Great Recession," unpublished working paper, University of California at Berkeley.

Nalewaik, Jeremy J. (2010) "The Income- and Expenditure-Side Estimates of U.S. Output Growth," *Brookings Papers on Economic Activity* Spring: 71-106.

Neiss, Katherine S. and Edward Nelson (2003). "The Real Interest Rate Gap as an Inflation Indicator," *Macroeconomic Dynamics*, 7, 239-62.

Okun, Arthur M. (1973). "Upward Mobility in a High-Pressure Economy," *Brookings Papers on Economic Activity*, 1973:1, pp. 207-252.

Orphanides, Athanasios (2003). "The Quest for Prosperity Without Inflation," *Journal of Monetary Economics*, 50(3): 633-663.

Orphanides, Athanasios and Simon van Norden (2002). "The Reliability of Output Gap Estimates in Real Time," *Review of Economics and Statistics*, 84(4): 569-583.

Orphanides, Athanasios and John C. Williams (2006). "Inflation Targeting Under Imperfect Knowledge," in *Federal Reserve Bank of San Francisco Working Paper Series* 2006-14.

Orphanides, Athanasios, Richard D. Porter, David Reifschneider, Robert Tetlow and Frederico Finan (2000). "Errors in the Measurement of the Output Gap and the Design of Monetary Policy," Journal of Economics and Business, 52(1/2): 117-141.

Poole, William (1971). "Alternative Paths to a Stable Full-Employment Economy," *Brookings Papers on Economic Activity*, 3, 579-606.

Ramey, Valerie A., and Matthew D. Shapiro (2001). "Displaced Capital: A Study of Aerospace Plant Closings," *Journal of Political Economy*, 109(5): 958-992.

Reifschneider, David, Robert Tetlow, and John C. Williams (1999). "Aggregate Disturbances, Monetary Policy, and the Macroeconomy: The FRB/US Perspective," *Federal Reserve Bulletin* 85 (January), 1-19.

Reinhart, Carmin M. and Kenneth S. Rogoff (2010). *This Time is Different: Eight Centuries of Financial Folly*. Princeton University Press (Princeton).

Sahin, Aysegul, Joseph Song, Giorgio Topa, and Giovanni L. Violante (2012). "Mismatch Unemployment," NBER Working Paper No. 18265.

Shleifer, Andrei (1986). "Implementation Cycles," *Journal of Political Economy*, 94(6): 1163-1190.

Stockhammer, Englebert and Simon Sturn (2012). "The Impact of Monetary Policy on Unemployment Hysteresis," *Applied Economics*, 44, 2743-2756.

Svensson, Lars E. O. (2003). "What is Wrong with Taylor Rules? Using Judgment in Monetary Policy through Targeting Rules," *Journal of Economic Literature* 41(2): 426-77.

Svensson, Lars E. O. (2005). "Monetary Policy with Judgment: Forecast Targeting," International Journal of Central Banking 1(1): 1-54.

Svensson, Lars E. O. and Robert Tetlow (2005). "Optimal Policy Projections," International Journal of Central Banking, 1(3): 177-207.

Taylor, John B. (1999). "A Historical Analysis of Monetary Policy Rules," in John B. Taylor, ed., *Monetary Policy Rules*. University of Chicago Press, 319-341.

Tobin, James (1972). "Inflation and Unemployment," *American Economic Review*, 62, 1-18.

Valletta, Robert G. and Katherine Kuang (2010). "Is Structural Unemployment on the Rise?" *Federal Reserve Bank of San Francisco Economic Letter* 2010-34 (November).

Valletta, Robert G. (2013). "House Lock and Structural Unemployment," *Federal Reserve Bank of San Francisco Working Paper Series* 2012-25 (April).

Yellen, Janet (2012). "The Economic Outlook and Monetary Policy," speech at the Money Marketeers of New York, New York (April 11), http://www.federalreserve.gov/newsevents/speech/yellen20120411a.htm

Appendix 1. The State Space Model

1. *Real GDP (per capita, logged)*

   gdp = wedge1 + tmfp/.965 + (.035/.965)*lveoa + .725*(terate + tlfpr + tww + wedge2)
   + .275*lks + .725*lqualt + cycle + β11*β6 + β11*e_nfbp + [white-noise error, var=β100^2]

2. *Real non-farm business output (per capita, logged)*

   nfbp = tmfp/.965 + (.035/.965)*lveoa + .725*(terate + tlfpr + tww + wedge2) + .275*lks
   + .725*lqualt + β10*cycle + β6 + e_nfbp

3. *Real non-farm business income (per capita, logged)*

   nfbi = tmfp/.965 + (.035/.965)*lveoa + .725*(terate + tlfpr + tww + wedge2) + 0.275*lks
   + .725*lqualt + β10*cycle − β6 + e_nfbi

4. *Workweek, nonfarm business sector (logged)*

   wwnfb = tww + 0.72*[wwnfb(-1)-tww(-1)] + φ20*[cycle-cycle(-1)] + φ(22)*cycle
   + [white-noise error, var=β104^2]

5. *Employment, nonfarm business sector (per capita, logged)*

   enfb = terate + tlfpr + wedge2 + φ30*cycle + φ31*[enfb(-1)-terate(-1)-tlfpr(-1)-wedge2(-1)]
   + [white-noise error, var=β105^2]

6. *Employment-to-population ratio (logged)*

   erate = terate + φ50*cycle + φ51*[erate(-1)-terate(-1)] + [white-noise error, var=β106^2]

7. *Labor force participation rate (logged)*

   lfpr = tlfpr + φ40*cycle + φ41*[lfpr(-1)-tlfpr(-1)] + [white-noise error, var=β107^2]

8. *Core PCE inflation*

   pcex = β401*pcex(-1) + (1-β401)*epi(-1) + β404*[.50*cycle + .33*cycle(-1) + .17*cycle(-2)]
   + β405*MA(rpe(-1),6) + β406*MA(d84*rpe(-1),6) + β408*rpm + β409*rpm(-1)
   + β407*wpc + [white noise error, var=β109^2]

   Note: MA(X,n) denotes the n-quarter moving average of X

9. *Business cycle (state variable)*

   cycle = β1*cycle(-1) + β2*cycle(-2) + [white noise error, var=β111^2]

10. *Nonfarm business output error (state variable)*

    e_nfbp = β602*e_nfbp(-1) + [white noise error, var=β125^2]

11. *Nonfarm business income error (state variable)*

    e_nfbi = β602*e_nfbi(-1) + [white noise error, var=β126^2]

12. *Trend level of the GDP-NFB output wedge (state variable)*

    wedge1 = wedge1(-1) + .25*gwedge1 + [white-noise error, var=β112^2]

13. *Trend growth rate of the GDP-NFB output wedge (state variable)*

    gwedge1 = .95*gwedge1(-1) + .05*β213 + [white-noise error, var=(4*.03326*β112)^2]

14. *Trend level of multi-factor productivity (state variable)*

   tmfp = tmfp(-1) + .25*gtmfp + [white-noise error, var= $\beta 114^2$]

15. *Trend growth rate of multi-factor productivity (state variable)*

   gtmfp = 0.95*gtmfp(-1) + 0.05*$\beta 214$ + [white-noise error, var= $\beta 115^2$]

16. *Trend NFB workweek (state variable)*

   tww = tww(-1) + .25*gtww + [white-noise error, var=.01]

17. *Trend growth rate of the NFB workweek (state variable)*

   gtww = .95*gtww(-1) + .05*$\beta 216$ + [white-noise error, var=$\beta 117^2$]

18. *Trend level of the wedge between household and NFB payroll employment (state variable)*

   wedge2 = wedge2(-1) + 0.25*gwedge2 + [white-noise error, var=$(.01*\beta 118)^2$]

19. *Trend growth rate of the wedge between household and NFB payroll employment (state variable)*

   gwedge2 = .95*gwedge2(-1) + [white-noise error, var=$\beta 119^2$]

20. *Trend level of the labor force participation rate (state variable)*

   tlfpr = tlfpr(-1) + 0.25*gtlfpr + [white-noise error, var=.0025]

21. T*rend growth rate of the labor force participation rate (state variable)*

   gtlfpr = 0.95*gtlfpr(-1) + [white-noise error, var=$\beta 123^2$]

22. *Natural rate of employment (state variable)*

   terate = terate(-1) + [white-noise error, var=$\beta 124^2$]

Exogenous variables

lveoa   trend energy-output ratio (logged)
lks   capital services (per capita, logged)
lqualt   labor quality (logged)
rpe   PCE energy prices relative to core PCE prices, weighted by energy share of consumer spending
rpm   non-oil import prices relative to core PCE prices, weighted by import share of domestic spending
wpc   wage-price controls (1971q3 to 1974q1 =1, 1974q2 to 1974q4 = -3.67, =0 otherwise)
d84   dummy variable (= 1 from 1985q1 on, = 0 otherwise)
epi   expected long-run inflation (as reported in the Survey of Professional Forecasters from 1990 to the present and in the Hoey survery from 1981 to 1990; prior to 1981 expectations are inferred by a trend extraction procedure using actual inflation)

Table A.1 Estimation Results for the State-Space Model (Sample period 1963:Q2 to 2013:Q1)

	Coefficient	Standard Error	z-Statistic	Probability		Coefficient	Standard Error	z-Statistic	Probability
β1	1.5165	0.0583	26.00	0.00	β126	0.4004	0.0369	10.84	0.00
β2	-0.5529	0.0593	-9.33	0.00	β213	-0.3378	0.0639	-5.29	0.00
β6	0.3115	0.3119	1.00	0.32	β214	0.8627	0.2705	3.19	0.00
β10	1.3896	0.0226	61.55	0.00	β216	-0.2079	0.1285	-1.62	0.11
β11	0.7193	0.0314	22.90	0.00	β401	0.5762	0.0643	8.96	0.00
β100	0.0586	0.0125	4.70	0.00	β404	0.0996	0.0279	3.57	0.00
β104	0.2147	0.0141	15.21	0.00	β405	0.5174	0.1859	2.78	0.01
β105	0.1619	0.0143	11.33	0.00	β406	-0.3467	0.3235	-1.07	0.28
β106	0.0819	0.0152	5.38	0.00	β407	-0.4646	0.1024	-4.54	0.00
β107	0.2126	0.0150	14.14	0.00	β408	0.3316	0.1452	2.28	0.02
β109	0.7605	0.0436	17.44	0.00	β409	0.2738	0.1778	1.54	0.12
β111	0.5702	0.0382	14.93	0.00	β602	0.9124	0.0328	27.78	0.00
β112	0.1254	0.0184	6.83	0.00	φ20	0.2511	0.0392	6.41	0.00
β114	0.2299	0.0539	4.27	0.00	φ22	0.0472	0.0132	3.57	0.00
β115	0.1361	0.0653	2.09	0.04	φ30	0.4518	0.0260	17.36	0.00
β117	0.0662	0.0276	2.40	0.02	φ31	0.6599	0.0249	26.53	0.00
β119	0.1142	0.0364	3.14	0.00	φ40	0.0427	0.0165	2.58	0.01
β123	0.1169	0.0306	3.82	0.00	φ41	0.7573	0.0883	8.57	0.00
β124	0.1359	0.0191	7.10	0.00	φ50	0.2933	0.0197	14.86	0.00
β125	0.5172	0.0405	12.76	0.00	φ51	0.5334	0.0336	15.87	0.00

Log likelihood	-610.625	Akaike info criterion	6.506253
Parameters	40	Schwarz criterion	7.165917
Diffuse priors	0	Hannan-Quinn criterion	6.773209

Appendix 2. Other Published Estimates of Potential Output

Like the real-time estimates generated by the state-space model, published estimates of potential output growth were revised down after the financial crisis, although the timing and the extent of these revisions varied considerably (Table A.2). The OECD and IMF adjusted down their estimates of potential growth quickly, and by sizable amounts, on the explicit assumption that financial crises are invariably followed by permanent supply-side losses. For example, the IMF slashed its estimate of potential output growth in 2009-10 from 2 percent to below 1 percent between late 2008 and late 2009. Although the incoming productivity data in the United States did not look particularly dark at first—and the IMF subsequently scaled back their estimate of the losses some—later vintages of NIPA data in the US came to validate the earlier IMF pessimism to some extent. For its part, the OECD lowered its estimate of potential output growth for 2009-10 to about 1½ percent in early 2009, where it has remained since. (Interestingly, both the IMF's and OECD's current estimates for potential growth in 2012 are 1¾ percent, noticeably above that from the state-space model.)   In contrast, U.S. officials were somewhat slower to recognize the decline in potential output growth. For example, the Congressional Budget Office did adjust down its estimate of potential growth from 2½ percent to 2 percent in August 2009, but it subsequently made further downward adjustments to its estimates for those years, in a pattern not unlike the vintage-based results from the state-space model. And the Council of Economic Advisers' estimate for those years was still at 2½ percent in 2010. The one private-sector forecaster we surveyed, Macroeconomic Advisers, also lowered its estimate of potential growth in 2009-10 relatively promptly to 1.2 percent by late 2009.

Appendix 3. Sensitivity of Supply-Side Estimates to Model Specification

Estimates of potential output and the natural rate of unemployment are sensitive to the particular model and procedures used to estimate them. We illustrate the importance of uncertainty about the proper specification of the state-space model by reporting the results from alternative versions that seem perfectly reasonable on their face. In particular, we estimate two versions with alternative specifications for inflation dynamics—one in which the coefficient on the common cycle term in the inflation signal equation is allowed to shift discretely starting in 1995, and another in which the inflation equation is dropped altogether. These two variations shed light on how the information content of inflation for slack may have changed in recent years.[52] In addition, we explore the sensitivity of our state-space estimates to the measures of output used in the model by considering a version that drops the signal equation for real nonfarm income.

As shown in the upper panel of Figure A.1, the inflation-related changes in specification do not markedly alter the estimated year-to-year movements in potential GDP growth (including the effects of level shocks). In contrast, as shown in the lower panel, the model's estimates of the natural rate are much more sensitive to changes in the inflation equation, as these changes result in either a modestly higher average level of U* (the result with a time-varying slope) or a much higher level (the result when the model does not condition on inflation at all). Estimates of the natural rate are also somewhat sensitive to the measures of aggregate output and income included in the state-space model, particularly prior to 2000. Moreover, and unlike the situation with the inflation alternatives, dropping nonfarm income from the model has a noticeable effect

---

[52] In the version of the state-space model that allows for a shift in the Phillips curve slope, the estimated coefficient on the cycle term drops markedly starting in the mid-1990s, falling to 0.04 from 0.16 prior to 1995.

on the estimated quarter-to-quarter pattern of potential GDP growth and, among other things, results in a somewhat higher estimate of trend growth in the past few years.[53]

Not surprisingly, frameworks that differ from ours in more fundamental ways can also yield different estimates of potential output and economic slack. To illustrate, Figure A.2 reports two alternative estimates of the output gap from the Board's DSGE model of the U.S. economy (EDO)—one a production-function measure comparable in spirit to that generated by the state-space model, and the other based on a Beveridge-Nelson statistical estimate of the long-run trend in aggregate capacity.[54] Compared to the baseline version of the state-space model, both of the EDO measures show a much narrower degree of economic slack in recent years, especially in the case of the production-function measure; this latter result largely reflects EDO's assessment that the trend in aggregate hours has fallen steeply since the middle of the 2000s. Yet another approach to estimating the output gap is that taken by Borio et al. (2013), who argue that adding information about the financial cycle to the state-space model yields more robust readings on aggregate resource utilization because doing so allows policymakers and others to take into account concerns about future financial imbalances; they also advocate ignoring inflation when filtering the data on the grounds that the Phillips curve has become too flat to be useful. Borio *et al.*'s measures imply much more damage to the supply side in recent years than do the estimates generated by our baseline state-space model.

---

[53] Fernald (2012) provides a different perspective on the uncertainty associated with empirical specification. Using a methodology that is similar to the CBO's but with different assumptions about underlying technology and capital growth, he finds a somewhat greater slowing in potential output growth following the financial crisis than does the CBO.

[54] For details on the current version of the EDO model (including the approaches used to estimate potential output), see Chung, Kiley and Laforte (2012). Also, see Beveridge and Nelson (1981), Clark (1987), and Haltmaier (2012) for a discussion of other applications of univariate time-series analysis to the estimation of trend output.

www.ingramcontent.com/pod-product-compliance
Lightning Source LLC
Chambersburg PA
CBHW080542290526
45790CB00006B/2515